CW00376143

Quarterly Essay

Quarterly Essay is published four times a year by Black Inc., an imprint of Schwartz Books Pty Ltd. Publisher: Morry Schwartz.

ISBN 9781760644222 ISSN 1444-884x

Subscriptions – 1 year print & digital auto-renew (4 issues): $89.99 within Australia incl. GST. Auto-renew outside Australia $134.99. 2 years print & digital (8 issues): $169.99 within Australia incl. GST. 1 year auto-renew digital only: $59.99.

Payment may be made by Mastercard or Visa, or by cheque made out to Schwartz Books. Payment includes postage and handling.

To subscribe, fill out and post the subscription card or form inside this issue, or subscribe online:

quarterlyessay.com
subscribe@quarterlyessay.com
Phone: 61 3 9486 0288

Correspondence should be addressed to:

The Editor, Quarterly Essay
22–24 Northumberland Street
Collingwood VIC 3066 Australia
Phone: 61 3 9486 0288 / Fax: 61 3 9011 6106
Email: quarterlyessay@blackincbooks.com

Editor: Chris Feik. Management: Elisabeth Young. Publicity: Anna Lensky. Design: Guy Mirabella. Associate Editor: Kirstie Innes-Will. Production Coordinator: Marilyn de Castro. Typesetting: Typography Studio.

In memory of Ingrid

LIFEBOAT

Disability, humanity and the NDIS

Micheline Lee

The world conspires to make us blind to its own workings; our real work is to see the world again.

Antoine de Saint-Exupéry

Last summer, my sister and I took our brother, who was visiting from Darwin, on a day trip to the Dandenong Ranges. My brother's disability support worker drove the van that we'd hired to fit all three of us in our electric wheelchairs in the back. As we curved up the hill, the sky obscured by tall mountain ash, our conversation flowed with fond memories of the trips we took here with our parents when they were still alive.

We stopped at a picturesque strip of shops popular with tourists. Rolling single file so we didn't block the footpath, we had to pass by one shop after another without being able to go in. None of the shops was accessible. All had at least one step. Finally, near the end of the street, there was a gift shop that we thought we might be able to enter. There were a couple of steps at the front entrance, but we noticed a step-less doorway to the side. It led to a courtyard full of artfully arranged pot plants, handmade gifts, mosaics and garden sculptures. As we entered, the customers in the courtyard stared or moved aside, or apologised for no reason.

My brother wanted to buy a gift to take back to his wife. He saw a hanging metal decoration and asked his support worker to take it down for him.

Since there were two steps into the main shop, he gave the support worker his credit card and asked her to make the purchase for him. The owner came out. He was swarthy, with greying hair that hung to his shoulders. Dressed completely in black, he could have been an ageing rockstar. "Good to see ya, mate," he said in a loud voice. He insisted that my brother take the piece for free. "Just seeing you out and about," he said, "you've made my day."

I could hear him from the other end of the courtyard. *Oh no*, I groaned, and tried to hide behind some pot plants. My brother was insisting that he pay. The owner, with a warm face and wide, gesticulating hands, responded that he had thought his business wouldn't make it through the Covid lockdowns, but "there's always someone worse off, and you've got to always help others!"

"And who are they?" He waved towards my sister and then, despite the pot plants, at me. "Can't leave them out, can we!" He stepped back into the shop. Before I had time to make a getaway, he was back and gesturing to my sister and me to come over. I felt conflicted and embarrassed but didn't want to hurt his feelings. I approached and gave him a smile.

"Good to see you smiling, and what a gorgeous smile it is," he said. He presented my sister and me each with a gift bar of soap. The other customers gave us fond, indulging looks.

As soon as we left the shop and were out of earshot, I muttered, "Aren't we just inspirational!"

My brother rebuked me: "You're too cynical."

"He was just being kind," my sister added.

"But it made you feel like a child, right?" I said.

"He's better than most people," she answered.

My brother's body had slid down the wheelchair on one side. The side supports on his backrest were not enough to keep him in place when the wheelchair jolted. We stopped at a space in front of a closed shopfront. His support worker supported my brother's head with the flat of one hand and pushed his shoulder with her other hand so he was sitting upright again.

She was an excellent support – kind, attentive and unassuming. I was grateful that she had been fine with helping me to the toilet during our day out, because it meant I didn't have to organise my own support worker.

My brother said he felt bad about getting the decoration for free when he probably earned more money than the shop owner. "Oh well," he added, "it makes him feel good."

"Exactly!" I said, "when what we need is people who will actually make real changes, like make their buildings accessible."

"Hey," my brother said, "let's go to the next shop and see what other free stuff we can score!" We all burst out laughing. My brother's support worker couldn't stop giggling. I loved my brother's wicked sense of humour but felt that he had effectively ended the conversation. I would have liked to talk more. You would think that having grown up together with the same disability, we would have shared our experiences more. We seldom did. This probably goes back to our history.

There were five of us siblings, all born in Malaysia. The two older ones were born without the condition. The three youngest of us were born with Spinal Muscular Atrophy. My father believed the three of us were the result of an ancestral curse. Ever since we were children, he would tell us the story of how his mother had been obliged by custom to live in the home of her husband's ageing parents and care for them. But she broke her duty and talked her husband into leaving his parents' home. On the day they walked out, her husband's parents slaughtered a pig and pronounced a curse upon the couple. I imagined this curse as a claw following my ancestors out the door. By a logic unbeknown to us, the curse bypassed one generation and my dozens of cousins and chose to sink its talons into my two siblings and me.

After we migrated to Australia, when I was about eleven years old, my parents became born-again Christians. Many people laid their hands on us in prayer and tried to raise us from our wheelchairs. "Demon of sickness," they would shout, "in the name of Jesus, leave the bodies of these children." There were always two or more prayer meetings or healing rallies every

week that we were forced to go to. Some of the congregants, without asking, would lay their hands on my head or my legs and start praying. Others
would first address me, "Do you want to be healed?" It felt churlish to say
no. But I didn't want to say yes – why did they think that I needed healing
any more than the next person? Soon I learnt to pretend that I couldn't speak
English so I wouldn't have to answer them.

A friend I've had since my schooldays came to a couple of those prayer
meetings with me. Recently, she asked whether growing up like that had
traumatised me. I said it had, a bit, but I had a better understanding of
my parents now. They had been told by doctors that our condition was
progressive and all our muscles would waste to the point that we would
not be able to move or breathe and we would die early. From infancy,
they saw how we weakened and would never meet the expected growth
milestones. This was their way of coping with our prognosis. We were
expected always to talk and act as though we were not disabled, as though
we were going to be healed. Today, our parents have both died, and my
brother, sister and I have lived beyond expectations and are now in our
fifties. But I still feel that constraint on sharing the experience of being
disabled with my siblings.

I wondered again about the rock-star shop owner and whether I was too
cynical, as my brother said. Perhaps I was still smarting from a previous
encounter, when I had enquired about wheelchair access to a gallery owned
by a popular patron of artists. The patron had replied, "If we have to put in
a ramp, then what will you ask for next, something for the deaf and blind?
It's not going to pay for itself, is it, and it's not like you people are going to
buy anything."

I did feel ashamed about criticising the shop owner when he was being
kind. Wasn't it empathy that led him to congratulate us for "getting out and
about"? After all, it had taken us a lot of effort and time to arrange for a
disability support worker and an accessible van, to ring around restaurants
to find a place where we could eat and to research where disabled access
toilets were available along the route. And too bad if I was tired and out of

sorts and just wanted to blend into the crowd. On my own, I would attract attention, but when it was the three of us people behaved like we were a spectacle! It was something I had to psych myself up for.

It was typical that people would stereotype us as either overcoming our disabilities (being inspirational) or letting the disability get us down (being victims).

"I don't see you as disabled," a work colleague once said, thinking she was complimenting me. "You and Theo [a mutual friend] have such different attitudes. You don't let your disability define you – you sit up straight with pride, but Theo just hangs his head."

I knew that Theo hung his head because of the weakened muscles in his spine. With the progress of my own disability, it may not just be a hang to my neck I'll be acquiring but also, to some, a negative attitude.

The problem, I suspected, was that the shop owner wasn't congratulating us for making the effort to go out into a world that is discriminatory and inaccessible. More likely, he was congratulating us for smiling or being positive despite being in wheelchairs. People think the problem is just your bodily or mental impairment. I'm not saying that pain and loss of function don't come with disability. My point is that people treat disability like it's a kind of strange and unnatural occurrence. But disabled or not, all our bodies shift and change and experience varying degrees of function and limitation. What many people don't see is the bigger issue: discriminatory attitudes and society's unwillingness to meet the needs of disabled people.

I wouldn't blame him, though. It can be hard to absorb the distinction between being limited by your own body and being disabled by society's barriers. It has taken me half a lifetime.

There were definitely a few positives about my parents' approach to disability. At a time when many parents would have sent us to a segregated school, I'm grateful that my parents sent us to our local state schools. The problem, though, was that these schools were full of steps and hard to get around. In primary school, the lack of access meant I had to stay in the classroom by myself every lunch and recess while the other children went out to play. It never occurred to me or any of the adults around that the school should have made changes or put in a ramp so that I could go out to play with the other children. When the classroom had emptied, I would take my sandwich and a big book of fairytales out of my desk. I read the tales from start to end, and then went back and read my favourites again. Of course, "The Little Mermaid" was my very favourite. Not the plastic Disney version – I loved the traditional version where she died.

"Every step you take will feel as if you were treading upon knife blades so sharp that blood must flow," said the sea witch as she held out to the little mermaid the potion that would change her tail to human legs. "Are you willing to suffer all this?"

"Yes," the Little Mermaid said in a trembling voice, as she thought of the Prince and of gaining a human soul.

Suddenly the bell would sound, and I would emerge from my watery depths. First, the clatter of running along the corridor, and then the kids bursting through the door, a game of chase started in the playground spilling into the classroom. And while the others filed back in, I'd sometimes catch snatches of excited talk or teasing, *he tried to kiss her behind the toilets*, or who can spin the longest; the room filled with their hot, flushed faces, chatter and laughter. It seemed so magical, this secret life of the playground.

In secondary school, I made my first friend, Frida. It was effortless, I looked at her drawings in art class and she looked at mine and we gravitated to each other. At lunchtime, she would stay in the classroom, and we would sit side by side and draw. Sometimes she would take me down the step in my wheelchair and push me into the playground. Our playground was also a car park, and one lunchtime while we were sitting there a van pulled up and out came a bustling woman wearing a white tracksuit.

"They're coming to take you away," Frida joked.

The woman did in fact come to get me. She operated a lift to load me into the van and took me to the disabled access pool at a school for children with disabilities. They helped me into bathers in a bathroom with lifting hoists and beds and bedpans, then lined me up with the others in wheelchairs by the side of the pool. There were four of us lined up, waiting for our turn to be taken into the water. I was second-last in line, and a teen a bit older than me was last.

Immediately, she beckoned to me. Her movements were big and erratic. Maybe that was why she had two seatbelts crisscrossing her torso. She didn't say words that I could recognise as such, but she made friendly expressive sounds, pointed at me and seemed to be asking my name. She was curious about me, as I was about her. Whether we understood exactly what the other was saying was hit-and-miss, but we enjoyed the exchange and continued until we got tired. The clock showed that we had been waiting for over an hour.

Finally, it was my turn to be taken into the pool. The water was deliciously warm and buoyant. My new friend, the last one still waiting, gestured to me from the side of the pool. She made swimming motions to me, and I pretended to splash her. "Your turn soon!" I called out.

But I had only been in the pool for a few minutes when a worker started to pull me out of the water. "The bus is here!" she said. Another worker was taking the brakes off my friend's wheelchair and dragging her away. She didn't even get the chance to feel the water.

She started to wail and thrash her body around. Her cry was agonising, her body jerked so violently that the wheelchair rocked. The worker who had been pulling me out of the water rushed over to her. Both workers pulled tight the belts around her, jerking her back. How many times had things like this happened to her, I wondered. Tears fell from my eyes. Her distress was unbearable. Suddenly I couldn't take it. A switch flicked in me, and I looked away from her. I tried to shut out her wails. *I will never be her*, I vowed to myself.

To my mind at that time, the solution was to not be disabled, to not be vulnerable. It did not seem that I could do anything about the way they were treating us. It did not occur to me to rail at them or that anyone would think what they were doing was wrong.

Disability was something I had to deny and overcome. This mindset influenced the way I tried to live right up until my twenties. I loved art but made myself study law because I knew I would need some power and money if I were to be able to fend for myself. There was no place for weakness in some of my legal jobs, and I would get pressure sores from sitting too long in one position rather than show that I needed help.

But my body could not be controlled. My motor neurons continued to die, my muscles wasted, and I got weaker. I fluctuated between ignoring my body and pretending it wasn't there; and watching it like a hawk. I measured small changes, repeated movements in timed brackets so I could compare how long I could go without fatiguing; kept notes of things that I could do six months ago which I couldn't do now. The future filled me with terror when I was young. *What will become of me when I get too weak to look after myself? Will anybody help care for me? Will there be a place for me in this world? Will I have any say in how I live my life?*

About thirty years later, in November 2012, I went online to listen to Prime Minister Julia Gillard introduce in federal parliament the bill that would create the National Disability Insurance Scheme. This bill would go on to receive bipartisan support and become Australia's largest social reform in a generation.

"The scheme to be established by this bill will transform the lives of people with disability, their families and carers," she said. "For the first time they will have their needs met in a way that truly supports them to live with choice and dignity."

The NDIS promised to provide disabled Australians with the "reasonable and necessary" supports needed to participate equally in society. Forms of support would include personal care, such as help with showering and feeding, assistance to go out into the community, domestic help, home access modifications, aids and equipment, and disability-related therapy, such as recovery coaching or occupational therapy. Individuals would be able to exercise choice and control over how they used their support to meet their goals in life.

Anyone under the age of sixty-five who had been assessed to have a significant and long-term disability that substantially reduced their capacity to live independently or take part in community life would be eligible. Alternatively, a disabled person could be eligible under the early intervention requirements, where early access to support would reduce their need for disability support in the future.

Previously, disability supports had been provided by the states and territories, and there was little consistency across different systems. Generally, though, the supports were underfunded, often inadequate and crisis-driven, and it was a lottery whether you would receive a service.

People with high need of support were living in institutions because they couldn't access the care they needed to live in the community. In some cases, young people with disabilities had no option but to live in aged-care homes to receive the support they needed. For those disabled persons living in the community, many had to rely on overstretched parents and family members because services were inadequate or unavailable.

The NDIS promised to help with deinstitutionalisation and to resolve these crisis situations, but it also promised to help with much more than basic care and survival. Disabled people would be assisted to participate in society. This might mean a support worker to help a person with an intellectual disability take part in a drama group, or for a person with a mobility disability to fly interstate for a conference, or the apps or devices needed by a person with a vision impairment to navigate their way through daily life.

At the time, I was living with my then partner and our twelve-year-old son. I was working three days a week as a legal adviser in a government department. I needed help with basic tasks such as getting out of bed and showering. Even with the support of my partner, who was also working, I was struggling to manage the tasks of daily living. I was unable to afford the expensive electric wheelchair, mobility aids and regular physiotherapy I needed. To buy the hoist that could lift me out of my wheelchair, I had to apply to a charity. Even though we both worked, these were not expenses we could afford on an ongoing basis. After I had been on a waiting list for three years and receiving ad hoc support from my local council, Victoria's state disability scheme provided me with a support worker for two hours every morning. While the administrators acknowledged it wasn't enough, they said this interim measure was all there was until someone else vacated their place on the scheme.

About three months before the introduction of the NDIS bill, I had tried to explain the scheme to Frida. We had remained close friends since that first year of high school in art class, and during uni we had been housemates. We both continued to love art: she drew all the time, mostly in black ink – fluid line designs and gorgeous funny cartoons when she was feeling well, and heavily scribbled faces and tangled forms when she was upset and anxious. She was gifted, technically polished and at times heartbreakingly expressive. With the right supports, Frida might have finished the fine arts course she had started and become a recognised artist. Frida had been involuntarily admitted to a psychiatric hospital for treatment for the first time when she was nineteen, and then every year or so since, except for a period of about six years when she had been in a stable relationship. In the last few years, the admissions had become more frequent.

Whenever I visited Frida in the secure mental health units, I was shocked to think that these places were supposed to be places of recovery. The rooms were cold and clinical, without plants, cushions or aesthetic softening of any sort. Staff were detached and watchful, and an edginess pervaded the air, as though chaos might break out, as it sometimes did. Frida hated going in, and the last few admissions had been particularly disturbing. She suspected me of getting her admitted and had started to see me as an enemy. I had never reported Frida for involuntary admission. Once, afraid she was about to harm herself, I had been tempted to make the call, but the knowledge that it would be police who would come to get her and the danger of that always stopped me. Repeatedly, Frida found herself forced in for treatment, then spat out again. There was no in-between support to help her in her daily life. Once she turned up at my doorstep unannounced. She had walked all the way from the hospital: they had discharged her without any follow-up and without so much as a train fare. Frida stayed a few nights, but in the end I couldn't cope and told her she had to go back to her own house.

That day, three months before the introduction of the NDIS, I went to Frida's flat. Frida opened the door in a frilly apron with flour all over her. I breathed out with relief when I saw that her expression was direct and warm. Fear and mistrust had poisoned our friendship in the last year. She had become more and more isolated from old friends, and we hadn't seen each other for a few months. But seeing her again was great: I felt all the old love for her and saw it shining back in her eyes. "I've been baking," she said, and laid out my portable ramp on the front doorstep to get me into her flat. We sat in her kitchen and chatted while she mixed the dough.

I moved the conversation on to the NDIS because I hoped it would help Frida and knew it would take a few months for her to warm to the idea.

I was pretty sure she would be eligible because of her schizophrenia diagnosis and suicide attempts since she was young. And I hoped she could get someone to help her in the periods when she was isolated and didn't look after herself. I explained that I would be getting support through the scheme when it commenced and suggested she also look into it. "To get on the NDIS, you have to show you have a permanent disability – this includes mental illness – and that you need disability supports to help you get on with life."

"It's obvious *you* need supports. I'm not going to lug you around without that wheelchair! But they're only interested in pumping me full of drugs."

"No, this isn't about medical care, it's about supports, and this time they're asking *you* what you need."

"Okay, Ms Micheline," she said, "you tell me. What do I need?"

"No, you tell me."

"Anybody ever tell you you'd make a good counsellor?" she said.

"Sorry for sounding like a counsellor," I said. "Want me to shut up?" She was silent.

"Well, what about help to get back to work?" I asked.

"Yeah, sure. But what can they do if no one wants to give me a job?"

Frida had worked most of her life in supermarkets and other retail, and for the most part loved it. I had witnessed her at work. She was great with and cared about her customers, she was quick with a joke and it was obvious her workmates and customers loved her. Frida never took a day off; she was always reliable – until she became unwell. Most of her bosses turned out to be intolerant and closed-minded when she needed some flexibility. As her unwell periods became more frequent, it was more difficult for Frida to pick up a new job when she lost one. Now it was about three years since her last job. It was a catch-22, because working was what helped keep her well. She felt worthwhile and part of the community when she worked. She had recently gone onto social security for the first time, but hated being on it. On the few days that she was well enough, she spent her time searching for work.

"So this is how the scheme will work," I said. "You tell the NDIS your goals in life and what disability supports you need to achieve those goals. And if they think those supports are what they call 'reasonable and necessary', you'll get those supports paid for. That means they don't cost too much and you need them because of your disability to achieve your goal. So you could tell them your goal is to find work and you need help with that – maybe someone who could help you negotiate flexible work hours with your boss."

"What, and tell an employer I'm a loony – are you kidding?"

"Some employers won't discriminate. They might even be helpful if they know what you need … Okay, what about a mental health coach who can help you deal with those days you're too anxious to get out of bed?" I could tell I was losing her.

"I want a man … and I need him to be decent and not a fucking prick," Frida suddenly said, with feeling. She rolled up the bread dough on the wooden board and started punching it.

"Of course you do." Suddenly I was filled with a sense of the futility of it all. Relationships, love and respect. That's what we ultimately wanted, wasn't it? Frida had always wanted her own family. Her partners had been abusive, taking advantage of her vulnerability. Except for one who in the end left her because she wanted a baby, but he didn't think she could raise a child. A mental health coach and disability supports might help you scrub up, but would that change the way the world rejected you?

"Look, I know what you mean, but the NDIS would be a good start – have a think about it."

"You can't always get what you want … but you get what you knead," she sang and laughed. Lifting up her elbows, she made a dramatic show of working the dough.

*

I put the volume up and turned my attention back to Prime Minister Gillard's speech. "This National Disability Insurance Scheme represents a transformational approach to the provision of disability services in this country.

Rather than attempt to patch and mend the existing system through further incremental change, we will build a new system from the ground up."

The NDIS was the culmination of decades of activism, along with an evolution in society's attitudes to the disabled. Every society has had cultural attitudes and values that have tended to dehumanise and disempower people with disabilities. For First Nations people of Australia, it has been suggested that disability may have been accepted as part of the human experience since there was no comparable word to "disability" in traditional languages, but disability was also viewed as cosmic punishment for breaking kinship rules and marrying "wrong-way." From my Chinese Malaysian background, I was seen as the result of a curse or a contamination to my lineage. I have experienced people still influenced by that tradition looking at me in repulsion and stepping clear of me.

In Australia, it's the Western view of disability which has dominated. Attitudes here were imported from Britain. Historically, people with disabilities in England were seen as possessed or moral degenerates, and ridiculed and humiliated. They were cared for by family, begged on the streets or found refuge in monasteries. With the introduction of the charity model in the 1600s, those unable to work were placed in poorhouses and given food barely adequate for survival under the principle of "less eligibility," since those on welfare were seen as not contributing to society and the economy.

From the early to mid-twentieth century, the eugenics movement led to the sterilisation of people with disabilities, and their segregation in cruel and inhumane institutions. After World War II, explicit eugenics policies came to an end. However, assumptions about the poor quality of life of people with disabilities still underlie medical practices aimed at preventing or ending the lives of people with certain disabilities. The medical model of disability saw disability as a defect, which needed cure or elimination.

The disability rights movement began around the 1970s, with the rise in the recognition of human rights. Demanding to be heard, activists challenged the dehumanisation of disabled people as objects of intervention. Institutions were seen as inconsistent with human rights and started closing down. Ideally, people would be taken care of in their own communities or at home, with help from government and not-for-profit organisations.

The social model of disability is said to be the disability rights movement's big idea. It originated in Britain in 1971 through discussions between two key people who had experienced the effects of segregation. They were Paul Hunt, a resident of a disability institution who led a protest against its restrictive conditions, and Vic Finkelstein, who had been expelled from South Africa for his anti-apartheid activities. The British social model redefined disability. It distinguished impairment from disability. Impairment is your biological or individual condition, while disability is structural and caused by the barriers and discrimination in society.

The social model is a direct challenge to the medical or individual model, which defines disability as individual deficit or tragedy and focuses on cure or therapy. The social model demonstrates that the problems people with disabilities face are the result of exclusion and social and environmental barriers such as discriminatory attitudes and policies, inaccessible buildings and transport, and inflexible work arrangements. They are not individual deficits. This places the moral responsibility on society to remove the burdens which have been imposed on disabled people, and to enable them to participate.

Since the 1980s, people around the world have been galvanised by the social model to advocate for more inclusive societies. It spurred the development of disability discrimination laws in many countries – including Australia's, in 1992. And, in Australia, it was fundamental to the development of the NDIS.

The simplicity of the social model makes it a powerful transformative tool, but it is not the whole story. It doesn't acknowledge that while impairment can be a source of pride, joy and creativity, it can also cause pain, severe limitation and death. In practice, what produces disability is the interaction of your condition or impairment with a social environment. For example, steps only keep you shut out if you have impaired mobility. Or systems that require the ability to enter into contracts only exclude you if you have a cognitive impairment. We are disabled by society as well as by our bodies.

The UN's Disability Rights Convention entered into force on 3 May 2008. Its drafting involved a high level of participation by people with disabilities, a level thought to be unprecedented for any previous human rights convention. Earlier human rights treaties had been premised on the liberal, autonomous, rational and self-sufficient person, who just needed to be protected from discrimination and interference in order to exercise their rights. The Disability Rights Convention recognised the artifice of that conception of the human. All people experience vulnerability and dependency to different degrees and at different life stages by virtue of our human and embodied state. The Convention moved away from the liberal conception of human rights to one that obliges states to remove barriers and take steps to achieve inclusion. States must recognise that people with disabilities have equal capacity to make their own decisions; and they must provide the supports needed to help the person make those decisions. It is not enough to have rights – you must have the real opportunity to exercise those rights on an equal basis. Society must also provide care and support.

The Disability Rights Convention sees disability as part of the human experience and variation, a normal part of life. It is not just an individual issue but a universal one. Policies should express this universality rather than cater only for people with a narrow range of ability. For example, in shaping the physical and social environment to accommodate human diversity, universal designers try to build public spaces with diverse needs in mind, including those of children, sick or disabled people, people from different backgrounds and the elderly.

Further, the Disability Rights Convention emphasises the need for the voice and lived experience of people with disability in all their diversity to be included in policy development. The social model and Disability Rights Convention have had a profound impact: they gave people with disabilities a way of calling for change that responds to our lived experience, rather than leaving us at the mercy of the assumptions of others.

*

The NDIS was yet to arrive, but already I had a feeling of optimism. For the first time, disabled people themselves and their families had a real say in creating the scheme. This time, it seemed different. Nothing about us without us.

One thing I knew was that society as it was did not give Frida the support and protection that she needed to flourish. Finding and keeping a job was nearly impossible once her mental illness became more severe and difficult to hide. The free market did not accommodate people who could not work in narrowly defined roles or at the same intensity.

Frida was inordinately proud of me. "This is my old schoolmate," she'd say when she introduced me to workmates or staff at the clinics she was admitted to. "She's a lawyer!" And when my partner and I adopted our son, she was even prouder. The introduction then became, "She's a mother and a lawyer!" It would often lead to laughter, as the person to whom Frida introduced me would inevitably say, "Hello, Mother and Lawyer!" At the same time, it made me wince to see her pride in me when I knew how much she wanted a child herself. I told her once how we had hidden the severity of my disability in our adoption application because most of the overseas agencies refused applicants with disabilities, and the only two agencies that didn't rule out disability altogether stipulated that only "mild" disability would be accepted.

"You shouldn't have to do that," she had responded. "Just stick it up them, tell them exactly who you are."

I didn't deserve any more praise than Frida did. Disabilities are as varied as people are, and the capacity to flourish in society depends mainly on how well you can assimilate. It's no coincidence that many of our most successful and respected disabled people are white men who are relatively able-bodied. Australian society works best for a narrow range of white, able-bodied, middle-class males. The further you are from this ideal, the harder it is to gain inclusion.

Until I was in my twenties, my focus was on fitting in, not only as a person with a disability but also as a Chinese immigrant. When I was at work,

I would go to the accessible toilet in the shopping centre half a kilometre down the street every time I needed to use the toilet rather than complain about the lack of wheelchair-accessible toilets in my building. There was little room for weakness in some of my legal jobs. A new client once rejected me as soon as he saw me. He told the manager that he needed a lawyer who would look the part in court. I just absorbed it, and instead of standing up for myself I felt ashamed.

It took relationships, and experiencing how diverse we all are, and a growing awareness and confidence, before I was prepared to acknowledge inequality and do something about it. Also, ironically, it helped that I became weaker and more dependent as my condition progressed. It wasn't the catastrophe that I feared when I was young. In fact, I was happier. You don't have to be perfect in body to experience the joy of a hug, a good book or a stunning sunset. I learnt that everyone has struggles and, ideally, we help each other. Suddenly, through experience, the social model of disability made a lot of sense to me. You can accept your disability. What is not acceptable is when the world treats you as second-class and excludes you because of it.

For some years, I represented people with disabilities in discrimination complaints. In Australia, the law has been our main tool for combating discrimination. Once, a client came in and said an insurance company refused him income protection insurance on the grounds that he had a vision impairment. It was a relatively easy case to make. This was because equal opportunity laws have an individual rights focus. They assume discrimination is caused by an individual who treats you unequally because of your disability. Most discrimination, however, flows from society's structures – an education system that is not adequately resourced to accommodate different learning needs or a criminal justice system that disadvantages people with cognitive disabilities. Therefore, the creation of the NDIS represented a great step forward in recognising the government's responsibility to remove barriers in society that prevent inclusion.

Growing up, I absorbed the message that my condition was a burden, the devil's work, and that I needed to be healed. From talking with other people with disabilities, I know that battling the shame of internalised discrimination is a common experience. The social model and the Disability Rights Convention helped me find a language to express that I was equal. It did that for many others too.

Though calls for a national disability support scheme started in the 1970s, concrete progress towards the birth of the NDIS only began in 2008, when the Disability Rights Convention came into force. At the time, I was working in a job unrelated to disability. I was just keeping my head above water with my other commitments as well as managing my disability. My involvement with the NDIS was to cheer from the sidelines or to contribute to submissions supporting the scheme.

In April 2008, Prime Minister Kevin Rudd called a two-day national summit, dubbed "The Australia 2020 Summit," at Parliament House. There were ten working groups of 100 participants each, and their goal was to help shape a long-term strategy for the nation's future. They were to discuss ten critical policy areas, including productivity, climate change and Indigenous Australia. Disability was not one of the areas included. Despite this, disability activists Bruce Bonyhady and Helen Sykes managed to get it onto the agenda through the side door by lobbying participants at the summit to raise the proposal for a lifetime care and support scheme. In response, in 2009, the Commonwealth government committed to consider such a scheme.

Also in 2008, the then Parliamentary Secretary for Disabilities, Bill Shorten, established an expert panel, the Disability Investment Group. He asked the group to explore innovative funding ideas from the private sector that would fund disability support for the future. The group included Bonyhady, who would be a key architect of the NDIS; he had had a career as a senior economist before getting involved in disability reform when he became the father of two sons with disabilities, and was chairman of Yooralla, a Victorian non-profit disabilities services organisation.

Having committed to the Disability Rights Convention, Australia promised to develop the first ever National Disability Strategy. To inform the strategy, disabled persons and families nationwide were asked to share their experiences. Disabled people and their carers talked of the barriers they encountered every day of their lives. Their message was simple – disabled people wanted to take part in the life of the community but were prevented because they were shut out. Compared to other OECD countries, Australia ranked lowest for the relative income of people with disabilities. They faced barriers to housing, education, healthcare, employment and recreation; they were twice as likely to be unemployed compared to people without disabilities, and many were isolated and segregated and experienced exploitation, violence and abuse.

As shocking as the situation was, this was not new information. What was new was their message that the disadvantage they experienced was not an inevitable consequence of their biological condition or impairments. They pointed to the poorly informed or discriminatory attitudes, the inaccessible buildings and public transport, the inflexible workplaces, the unaccommodating legal system and inadequate disability support services. And they called for change.

The NDIS was not the only urgent priority. School education was and still is failing disabled children and youth, and creating a segregated system. But strategically, it was more powerful to focus on one issue. It was decided that the focus should be on disability supports, because this area had been dysfunctional for decades and the need was urgent.

The idea of a national compensation scheme to meet the needs of people with disabilities was first raised in 1972, when Gough Whitlam was prime minister. He commissioned an inquiry, which recommended a national framework of support. The idea died with Whitlam's dismissal, but the agitation by people with disabilities who sought recognition for their rights had only just begun.

The Disability Investment Group submitted its report in September 2009. It recommended a feasibility study into a long-term scheme. The Productivity Commission subsequently conducted this study, releasing a report in 2011. It recommended that a national disability insurance scheme be introduced to provide cover for all Australians in the event of disability. As it pointed out, there were a wide variety of disability support programs fully or partially funded by state or federal government. These were highly complex and uneven in the level of support provided, and varied depending on where you lived, the kind of disability you had and various other factors, and had little or nothing to do with real need. The Productivity Commission's focus was on questions of efficiency, and it recommended a complete overhaul of the existing system.

By this time, disability activists had organised themselves into a highly effective grassroots alliance. They asked for three main things from a disability support scheme. First, it had to operate as a right; second, disabled people should have the right to manage their own lives and decide themselves what supports they needed; and third, the supports should enable them to participate on an equal basis in economic, social and cultural life.

Right, not charity

Crucially, the disability supports had to be a right so that they did not depend on the budgetary priorities of the government of the day. Only this would give the assurance that adequate support would continue for as long as the person needed it. Underwriting this was the principle of equal recognition. Disability supports are not a form of charity. Governments need to govern for all and ensure every person has an equal opportunity for inclusion.

In response, the NDIS promised a new way of providing disability supports. It would operate as an entitlement to "reasonable and necessary" support, enshrined in national legislation, for those who needed it.

As a world-first, the NDIS would work as an insurance scheme, which, it was claimed, would ensure financial sustainability. It would not be insurance in the sense that users pay a premium for coverage. Rather, the NDIS is insurance provided by the government to protect everyone from the costs and exclusion of a major disability, which could happen to anyone. Under the scheme, funding would be based on individual need rather than on an arbitrary budget cap. The scheme would be universal by virtue of three tiers of support the NDIS promised to deliver.

Tier 1 would benefit all Australians, both by providing them the assurance that if they were to acquire a disability, they would be supported for the rest of their life, and by helping create a more inclusive society.

Tier 2 would support all people with disabilities (about 4.8 million people or almost one-fifth of Australia's population), regardless of whether they were eligible for the scheme, by ensuring access to mainstream services, such as health, employment and education, and through local community groups, such as mental health support groups. Roughly 90 per cent of this cohort would not be eligible for individual NDIS support packages and would rely solely on Tier 2 services for assistance.

Tier 3 would provide individual support packages to individuals under the age of sixty-five whose disability needs were the greatest (persons with permanent and significant disabilities causing significantly reduced functioning in self-care, communication, mobility and/or self-management, and who required ongoing support). In line with the insurance approach, individual packages would also be provided to those whose level of disability itself might not qualify them for support, but for whom early intervention, including in early childhood, would be likely to reduce their future need. It was estimated that these two Tier 3 cohorts would comprise around 475,000 people.

Choice and control

Next, people with disabilities had called for a scheme that would allow self-management and the right to make their own decisions. They wanted supports that would respond to their diversity and that they could tailor to their own needs and goals. Disabled people are as diverse as humanity. Types of impairments are diverse and come with their own accompanying strengths and needs. Added to that, disabled people's race, gender, sexuality, age, education, religion, economic and social class bring further variability to the mix. And yet it had been seen as acceptable to treat them in a one-size-fits-all manner.

A few states had begun to give disabled persons some direct control over how they used their support funds, but generally previous schemes used block funding, which went to service providers, who had the power to decide what supports to allocate and to whom. Some providers would allocate supports according to their own criteria, without proper consideration of what the person needed or wanted.

The problems included that services for Indigenous people were often culturally inappropriate and disabled people living in remote communities would have to leave their homes and communities to live in larger towns to obtain support. Some service providers wouldn't provide support workers past 9.30 pm. One of my friends would have to sleep in her wheelchair if she ever wanted a late night out. Some people who relied on help for showering had no control over what time or how often they could take a shower. When my son was a baby, I needed some help bathing him, but the service provider made a senseless demarcation that the support worker could only help me with my personal care and not in my role as a mother. Some service providers were refusing to help people dress in the way they chose.

In response to disabled people's call for self-management, the NDIS promised them "choice and control in the pursuit of their goals, and the planning and delivery of their supports." The Productivity Commission recommended that the NDIS provide this choice and control through individualised funding. People with disabilities would decide themselves how they spent their support budgets to best meet their needs and goals. Instead of expecting people with disability to fit into existing programs and services, it was hoped that services would respond to the choices of people. It was assumed that individualised funding would achieve a structural shift in power, providing participants with a degree of control that many would never have experienced before.

Participation, not isolation

The third element that disabled people called for from the NDIS was also the ultimate goal of the scheme. It was to take part in economic, social and cultural life. Disabled people wanted more than just survival, getting out of bed, showering and eating, and maintaining basic health. They wanted support to participate and to create the lives they chose – to come out of isolation, to live in the community, work, make friends and pursue interests like other people. To this end, the Tier 2 goal of the NDIS was to make "mainstream services and community organisations become more inclusive of people with disability." Of course, this would not be a task for the NDIS alone.

The goals of the scheme were about advancing the human rights of disabled persons. The crucial question became: how do you turn human rights goals into effective policies and practical realities? The disability support system had been seriously underfunded and needed at least a doubling of funds (an additional $6.5 billion per year) to achieve the goals for which people with disabilities had advocated. It was predicted many would receive more funding than before and many would receive funded support for the first time.

However, to gain bipartisan support, the proponents needed to come up with a scheme that could demonstrate a strong business case – an economic justification, in other words.

A large part of the scheme's economic justification was the insurance approach. The idea for providing disability support as insurance was influenced by accident schemes such as workers' compensation or motor vehicle compensation. These had evolved in the 1980s to focus on rehabilitation and prevention and were governed by an independent statutory authority. Bruce Bonyhady said the "light-bulb" moment came for him when he talked with Brian Howe when Howe was the deputy prime minister, and he had advised him to view disability policy as risk insurance and investment rather than welfare. As Bonyhady explained, under the "welfare approach" to disability services, "Governments plan for expenditures over a twelve-month period to – at most – a five-year time frame ... as a consequence, the funds available for disability can change – depending on the economy, tax revenues and the requirements of other portfolios." In contrast, under an insurance approach, "expenditure is factored in over the life of an individual – and scheme sustainability is measured by calculating the total future costs of all those who are insured." Bonyhady argued that this would create an incentive to make short-term "investments" in participants aimed at increasing their independence and participation in the hope of reducing long-term costs.

The insurance approach ties into a neoliberal liking for a "business case" based on economic incentives. It is based on the principle that short-term investment in people's capacities would bring longer-term economic returns. In 2011, the Productivity Commission found that the benefits of the NDIS – in the form of increased employment of people with disabilities – would outweigh the costs and would by 2050 add almost 1 per cent to Australia's GDP.

I worried about the business premise. No amount of investing in the individual is going to increase a person's chances of finding a job if the transport they need to get to work is inaccessible or the employer has discriminatory or inflexible attitudes. For increased participation, a lot more needed to be done than investing in the individual. With its Tier 2 changes, the NDIS was promising to foster the broader changes needed to make society more accessible – however, there was a distinct lack of detail.

I worried too about the lack of detail on choice and control over services. Individual funding alone would not buy the disabled person more agency. People would still need assistance to access and manage services. People with severe cognitive disabilities would need help to make decisions. And having real choice required the availability of real options. There needed to be, for example, accessible housing, properly trained support workers, availability of disability supports in remote Indigenous communities and so on.

But I put aside my misgivings in the face of the vastness of the achievement of the NDIS. It was rare to see laws being passed of this import, cost and scale. What was being created was a whole new national structure as big as Medicare. For the first time, the provision of disability supports was being treated as a right. The goals in themselves demonstrated a cultural shift, an acknowledgement of collective responsibility to prevent discrimination and exclusion; and that both individual supports and removal of social barriers were needed to allow inclusion.

I felt so grateful to the disability activists and politicians who had fought for the NDIS, and for the goodwill that many Australians had shown towards the scheme.

But it was only the beginning. All we had so far were goals and designs, and everything would depend on implementation. Those responsible for this would need to recognise disabled people as equals and understand how society's structures are at the root of their unequal treatment. Disabled persons led the charge for the creation of the NDIS, and it was vital that they should also lead the implementation.

The NDIS came too late for Frida. She took her own life a month before the legislation was introduced. My mind kept going over the same things, trying to make meaning out of it. It was the loneliness; her friends and I should have done more; if only she could have kept on working; if only there had been the support she needed to keep on working; if only society hadn't treated her like a pariah; if only ... if only ...

Prime Minister Gillard came to the end of her speech: "It will change our society in profound and lasting ways, enabling those who live with disability to fulfil their potential as valued and valuable members of our society."

Every word she uttered seared into me. Could the NDIS really create a more caring and inclusive society?

In July 2013, the NDIS was launched as a three-year trial at several sites across Australia. At the end of the trial in 2016, the NDIS commenced its national rollout and by 2020 had replaced all the old state disability systems. The launch had been brought forward by a year, meeting a political imperative to secure the NDIS before the September 2013 federal election. Just months after the Labor government introduced the NDIS Act, the Coalition government took and held power for the first nine years of the scheme.

It's more than ten years now since the NDIS was launched. Almost 600,000 disabled people are receiving individual funding packages for disability supports. More than half of the people on the NDIS had never been eligible for support under the old system. For those who can access the scheme and turn funds into the support they need, the NDIS is, as many have said, life-changing. I've had an individual funding package – or, in NDIS-speak, I have been a participant – for about five years. Without the NDIS, I wouldn't be able to pay for the support workers I need to live independently in my home. This was crucial for me after my partner and I separated two years ago and my son moved away for his studies. For the first time I am living alone.

In other ways, the scheme has not delivered what it promised. For many, it has not provided choice and control in how we manage our support, nor better inclusion in society. Significantly, the scheme itself is inequitable and gains for some disabled people have been accompanied by hardship for others. They're teething problems, or "a plane launched before it was fully built," some said – but the faults, as it turned out, go deep into the design of the scheme.

Disabled people played a central role in the instigation and initial policy development of the NDIS but were shut out of the implementation. The NDIS is administered by an independent statutory agency called the National Disability Insurance Agency (NDIA). The NDIA board oversees the NDIS and makes its strategies and policies. A Ministerial Council, comprising ministers from the Commonwealth government and the states and territories, makes recommendations. And the Commonwealth minister is responsible for administering the NDIS Act.

Disability activists called for a majority of disabled people on the nine-member board, but the federal government appointed only two: advocate Rhonda Galbally and actuary John Walsh. Further, the government removed Bruce Bonyhady, the inaugural chair of the NDIA board, and replaced him with the chairperson of a large credit company, who had no lived experience of disability. Bankers and corporate representatives whose priority was economics were placed in charge of the scheme, and the experiential knowledge of disabled people was devalued.

The NDIS is jointly funded: the Commonwealth is responsible for just over half the cost and the rest comes from the states and territories. Funds from an increase to the Medicare levy from 1.5 to 2 per cent also contribute. However, when it comes to any scheme overspend that goes beyond the agreements, the Commonwealth government is solely responsible.

Early in the scheme's implementation, another decision was made by the federal government that would reduce the capacity of the NDIS. Intent on cost-cutting, the government focused on reducing short-term upfront costs. That has compromised the ability of the NDIS to flourish. In 2014 the government capped NDIA staff at 3000, less than half the number recommended by the Productivity Commission for effective operation. A 2017 commission report found the cap potentially led "to poorer outcomes," and that this was so "especially early in the scheme's life when the agency is building capacity and institutional knowledge, and developing first plans for many participants."

Access to the NDIS

NDIS processes are complex and obscure and hard to navigate, even for people seasoned in bureaucracy. Most participants have some form of cognitive disability, so it's important that processes take this into account. However, participants say the NDIA lacks even the fundamental elements of contemporary customer service.

Every participant in the NDIS is given an annual plan that sets out the "reasonable and necessary" supports that will be funded for that year. Criteria include that the support is disability-related and will assist social and economic participation. The support cannot be part of day-to-day living costs or be something another government department, such as health or education, should be providing. The support should also be effective, beneficial and value for money.

The plan is supposed to be drafted jointly with a planner and give the disabled person choice and control. The plan is a big deal. If a support is not clearly covered by a plan or explicitly listed, then it won't be funded. In my first plan, for example, the cost of repairs to my disability equipment wasn't listed. So when my wheelchair broke down halfway through the year, this cost wasn't funded.

The planning process is notoriously disempowering. The plan is usually developed in one phone conversation with a planner. Each year you are likely to get a different planner. You don't get to see or comment on what the planner has written in your plan before it goes to an anonymous NDIA decision-maker for final approval. If the approved plan contains mistakes, the NDIA won't adjust it. Any adjustment requires a full plan review, for which you may have to wait several months or more. Every year, weeks before my planning meeting, I am fearful. Everything depends on the planner you are allotted that year, and whether they have any understanding of disability and are responsive to who you are and your needs.

At my second planning meeting, the planner advised, "The aim is to have a higher investment at first that will decrease as you become better or more independent. This means that the funding in your next plan should be reduced."

"Well, I'm not getting better, my condition is progressive. If anything, I will need more supports each year, not less," I said.

There was a pause on the other side of the phone. "This is an insurance scheme," she said coolly. "We need to follow the insurance approach."

"You're talking to a real person," I said exasperated, "not someone who has to fit into one of your boxes!" My plan was arbitrarily reduced that year. I read with dismay the news that a scientist with a progressive disability was denied funding for a wheelchair and home modifications on the basis of his expected degeneration.

NDIA planners and decision-makers are in many cases insufficiently resourced and trained. I spoke with B, who had a NDIA-outsourced job to approve disability equipment and home modifications. "The requested item is first referred to an occupational therapist or relevant expert," he said, "but then their expert recommendation is ignored and it goes back to the NDIA for the final approval because it wants to cut costs. It was absurd! I saw some bad decisions being made ... we had no idea. Especially about home mods. And the delays can be awful. I had a client who died last week. He waited a year for an electric wheelchair. The day after he died, it was approved."

The NDIS is an uncapped scheme that aims to respond to need. At the same time, the NDIA is tasked with managing the financial sustainability of the scheme and aims to control spending by limiting who gets an individual package and how big it is.

Participants complain that the "reasonable and necessary" criteria are inconsistently applied and there isn't a shared understanding of their interpretation. It is also known that the NDIA uses an automated decision-making process involving actuarial tools as a guide to plan sizes, but the detail of this is hidden from participants.

Disputes about eligibility for the scheme and whether a support will be funded have seen record numbers of cases and long delays in the Administrative Appeals Tribunal (AAT). Many of the tribunal's decisions that apply the reasonable and necessary criteria concentrate on whether the support is beneficial and value for money. Finding a consistent thread in decisions is difficult. The purchase of a $12,000 swivel car seat that enables a person to get into their car independently was found not to be reasonable. The AAT took into account that there was a cheaper option for getting into the car, even though this alternative would require the help of others. The purchase of an all-terrain four-wheel-drive wheelchair for a person with a deteriorating condition was found to be reasonable and necessary; but the purchase of a new orthotic attachment that would allow a woman to wear high-heeled and not just flat-heeled shoes was not allowed.

In some cases, the participant is funded to have a support coordinator who assists in developing a plan and organising services. However, a support coordinator with relevant experience is hard to find and there is little information available that would assist in determining their suitability. There are no formal qualifications for the role and the coordinators vary greatly in experience, knowledge and quality.

Jessie is a disability advocate living in regional New South Wales whom I came to know recently. She has two beautiful children, the younger of whom, Mindy, has a severe cognitive and physical disability requiring 24-hour care. Fifteen-year-old Mindy is at constant risk of seizures and choking and can't eat any solids.

I don't think I have ever seen Jessie relaxed. Even when we meet and chat in a café, her eyes dart around on high alert, her body taut and ready to spring into action. One time we were about to go for a drive in my car, but it was acting up. She was direct with me: "If there's a problem with your car, I'm not getting in. I can't afford to have any accidents or have anything ever happen to me. I have to be here for Mindy."

It has been a fierce battle for Jess to get the support that Mindy needs. Mindy had her first plan in 2013, during the trial period. At first the NDIS planner gave her a plan that made no sense. "We had no idea what the plan meant or how to use it. The planner wrote that we needed walking aids rather than a wheelchair. I took Mindy into the NDIS office so the planner could see that she couldn't walk. She wouldn't help, she stopped taking my calls.

"Mindy's health declined every year. The gap between what she needed and what she got became wider. At first, I didn't have a clue how to advocate. When a door closed, I didn't understand you could disagree or ask for a review." Jessie had grown up disadvantaged, with a disrupted education, but as she said, she had to learn quickly. "At first I hated the NDIS because it provided a picture that life was better but there was no support there. I felt that I would never get it. I didn't know about support coordinators and it was hard to get through to the NDIS phone enquiries."

Finally Jessie asked for a meeting with the most senior planner. When he wouldn't help, she told him she was going to relinquish Mindy and he'd better take her straight to the hospital. She started to walk away. Jessie said she would never have done that, but it was her last resort. The planner grabbed hold of her and apologised, and finally started to listen. Since then, Mindy has had a plan that generally meets her funding needs.

Having the funding was only the first step. As Jessie recounted, "We started with an agency and were given unskilled workers with no disability experience, who were just task-oriented. There was no opportunity to interview the workers. Since I invested a lot of time training my own support workers, the NDIS is helpful to me. It is helpful that I now have a complex care planner at the NDIA who I can contact. I can achieve good support by intensive training and putting up posters and signs and manuals. Mindy is like someone who speaks a different language. She can't say what she needs. You have to learn her language. You do that through me. But workers keep coming and going, and I can't afford to have to do it ongoing. Having to constantly train new workers means I can't do my own work."

To Jessie, it's attitude that makes the difference. The attitudes of the NDIA planners and decision-makers and especially the support workers. "The support workers are the face of the NDIS," she said. Jessie said she's thankful now for the scheme, but fears what would happen if she wasn't there to advocate for her daughter and to manage and train the workers herself.

Access to the market

Jessie and Mindy's experience of having to fight for the supports they needed is related to the fact that the NDIS was set up as a market system with minimal market stewardship. The participant is supposed to be able to exercise choice and control in this system through empowerment as a consumer. I didn't realise the full implications of this until 2017, when I heard about

Francis. He was a twenty-year-old man with an intellectual disability who, according to his Legal Aid lawyer, loved trains and his iPad. He lived in his residential unit and had an NDIS package to pay his disability service provider for the 24-hour high-needs care he required.

Francis committed a minor assault for which no one would end up in prison, particularly someone like Francis with no history of offending. Yet Francis ended up spending a total of 180 days in prison, mostly in solitary confinement for his own protection. The magistrate said he was not able to let Francis go because he didn't have the disability supports he needed to return home. Francis's service provider, describing him as a "business risk," had refused to care for him, and no other agency would accept him. Legal Aid sought the help of the NDIA in finding a provider of "last resort" for Francis. But the NDIA denied responsibility, saying it was "just a bank."

By the time a suitable provider had been found so that Francis could return home, the experience in prison had so badly traumatised him that his home had to be modified to provide a prison-like enclosure in which he could feel safe.

Francis's situation was not unusual. More reports were emerging of people with complex support needs ending up homeless, in emergency wards or in prison because no support provider would accept them. Under the old model, they would most likely have received care in a state-run group home. Under the new regime, private providers have simply withdrawn support when the person exhibits challenging behaviours. There is no provider of last resort, nor any structure to ensure a person actually receives the support they need.

This wasn't the NDIS we had fought for. Individualised funding was from the start a significant component of the Productivity Commission's recommendations, but we did not sign up to a scheme where an individual is left to sink if they don't fit the image of the ideal consumer. Individualised funding has worked well in other countries, where it exists within an ecosystem of structured supports. These include the strong involvement of government and local support organisations, as well as informal supporters to ensure continuity of care; training and accountability of staff built into the system; and "intermediary" services to assist individuals in planning and managing how money is used.

The NDIS transition to a market-based system, however, saw an abdication of federal, state and territory responsibility to be a provider of last resort. Despite decades of evidence of how these markets fail, the implementers, particularly in the early days of the scheme, adopted a classic market system. They were reluctant to supplement the free market with public service provision or the contracting out for specific services that were missing from the market. This approach saw the erosion of vital networks and structured supports within the community. Rather than the NDIS setting up the structures needed to ensure support, properly trained workers and intermediaries, adequate safeguards, the advocates, the community visitor and so on, most of this responsibility has fallen to the individual.

According to the designers of the scheme, this is how the NDIS system should work. The NDIA provides some stewardship – for example, incentives for the market to expand quickly, or the imposition of price caps – but minimal government involvement is favoured. The government withdraws from delivering services. Its role, as bureaucrats say, is to "steer, not row." "Central to the Scheme is a shift to directing funding and resources to Scheme participants who will then drive and shape the market (just as in many other commercial markets) through their individual choices of the providers to deliver the supports in their plans." The NDIS explains that "People with disabilities are consumers and it is through their role as consumers that they will be able to exercise choice and control over their service provision." On the supply side, providers will enter the market driven by the profit motive to compete and deliver individualised customer services. Competition among customers will drive down costs and ensure the quality of service is high.

That was the theory. It is not what has happened in practice. First, there are too few customers – what are called "thin" markets – to attract profit-seeking service providers. The Productivity Commission assumed that demand would stimulate supply wherever it was needed. But rather than shifting to where they are most needed, services have tended to shift to where they can be delivered – and therefore profits made – most easily. Those living in remote and regional areas and those who have complex needs requiring specialist services have been especially affected by severe shortages of services.

The assumption was that competition among private providers would make services cheaper and better. The opposite is the case. Providers have raised their prices, taking advantage of situations where there is more demand than supply and NDIS money is available. Once they know you are on the NDIS, many providers will charge the maximum rate allowable under the scheme. Since the NDIS, I have generally found disability equipment prices to have shot up, fewer providers will do any customisation and some providers are imposing requirements that would not ordinarily be acceptable. The company I use for wheelchair repairs now has a policy that you have to pay the full amount quoted upfront before they will even schedule an appointment, even if it is six months from now. If you complain about unfair practices, it's at your own cost, as I found out when I was put at the back of the queue.

I am one of those who has benefited from the NDIS. Without it, I would not have been able to afford the daily personal care I need to stay in my own home. Yet recruiting suitable support workers is difficult. Many agencies have no availability, so I have to resort to the Uber-style platforms where you do all the managing of the worker yourself. On these, many workers show a preference for "community access" jobs that involve accompanying clients to shops, workshops, movies or other outings. The work I require doesn't generally involve community access. Because of the shortage of workers, it's they who can pick and choose, rather than the person seeking support.

It can take me several days to several months of seeking and interviewing to find a new worker. I provide training to them on the job, and it usually takes about six months before they become familiar with how to handle my assistive equipment and me.

I see my relationship with my support workers as an intricate dance. My needs are quite specific, millimetre-specific, in fact, as my occupational therapist says. I teach them the steps, they need to respond to my moves, learn which of my hands is stronger, where I need to be held so I don't fall, how to place objects so I can reach them. They need to put aside their preconceptions of how I should dance, but when they know my steps, then it flows and they can add value and suggest new ways of doing things. And then they leave and I start the process all over again.

What makes my situation more complex is that though I need a high level of physical assistance, I try to continue doing as many things on my own as I possibly can, like transferring from my wheelchair to my bed, even when there is the risk of falling. I keep the support work to a minimum as I value having time to myself. With the old system, I would have been in danger of being put into more restrictive care, but under the NDIS there is no such oversight.

Similarly, under the old system, as my disability progressed, the equipment authorities decided my small home scooter was not stable enough for me and posed an unacceptable risk. They refused to maintain it. Now, under the NDIS, I still can't find a provider to maintain it, but for a very different reason. Whereas under the old system they were presuming to make a decision for me in my best interests, in the privatised world of the NDIS no provider will touch my scooter because the specialisation required in the customisation means there's not enough profit in it.

Not-for-profits and providers who prioritise training and advocacy and working with the client's family and social networks have found it more difficult to survive in this individualised "fee-for-service" market environment. Some types of care require more training and investment than others. Many private providers are interested only in the most lucrative participants. Those whose needs are more complex, who require support workers with more expertise or a larger upfront investment, will find few options available. Or in some cases, private providers will take on clients with complex needs and simply overlook the need for expertise until an incident occurs.

Lou, a support worker in her early twenties, took her first disability-related job with an agency that formed in response to NDIS demand. Lou told me she had no care-related work experience whatsoever and thought she would receive some training. The agency, however, provided no training except for a thirty-minute NDIS-produced video that they told her to watch in her own time. After she had been at the agency for only a couple of months, the manager asked her to work with a new client who, he said, could be "a bit difficult." The manager would give no further information, but then, as Lou said, they were never given any information about their clients and what their needs were, just shift locations and times. On the first two shifts, N, her client, wanted Lou to drive her to the shops and to a park. Lou understood that she was to do most of the interacting with shop personnel on N's behalf, but often she couldn't understand what N was saying, and this would make N very frustrated. On the third shift, while they were at the park, N threatened to throw herself down a steep embankment. When Lou approached N to hold her back, N stepped closer to the edge and warned Lou to keep away. Lou rang her manager, who told her to ring the police. The police asked for details but Lou could only give the police N's first name and address, which was all she knew of the person she was supposed to be caring for. An hour later, the police hadn't come and it was getting dark. N finally stepped away from the embankment and asked Lou to drive her home. Lou said all the time she was scared and "out of my depth." She said that, after the incident, the agency "dumped" N.

The quality of support workers is crucial to good outcomes, yet this has been compromised by lack of training and low retention rates. Many people with psychosocial disabilities see "recovery" as the main aim of mental health services. By recovery, the focus is not on clinical recovery so much as on living a meaningful life – including in the community, with or without symptoms. Those whose aim is recovery need help in taking more control and managing the complex challenges of day-to-day living, but workers trained to do this are in short supply. People with severe intellectual disabilities need active support, not just being sat down in front of the television.

Research shows these people being disengaged for twenty-two minutes out of each hour. They are much more likely to be seen as a non-person when disengaged.

Even if the problem of thin markets were not a reality, not everyone can be the "ideal consumer." NDIS participants still face obstacles to getting support if they can't advocate for themselves or don't have someone to advocate for them. The designers didn't take into account the different capabilities of individuals to transform their funds into the ability to buy services, much less to participate in wider life.

Central to the market model is the assumption that the participant can choose to go elsewhere in search of a better service once they become aware that the service they are receiving is not good enough. This is assumed to drive out inefficient or substandard providers. There is some truth in this for services with a large demand. The problem is that there is no information available by which participants can assess which providers give a better service. Further, disabled people have a broad range of needs and circumstances. The more complex the service, the greater the risk of moving from one service to another and the more difficult it is to find another equivalent service, or indeed find a service at all.

The perfect storm of thin markets, NDIS complexity, bureaucracy and lack of structural supports, and the compounding difficulties of linguistic, cultural and literacy barriers, come together in First Nations remote communities. Mona lived in one of the Utopia homelands about 255 kilometres into the desert country east of Alice Springs. For about a year, she worked as a coordinator and one of her roles was to assist disabled members of the community to access support under their NDIS plans. She said that most of them had not even seen their plan, had no idea what was in it and didn't know where to start. But there was one community leader, K, who had some understanding of the NDIS through her son, and Mona introduced me to her. K's 32-year-old son lives with a mental health condition. She told me that the treatment and support her son needed were not available in his community, so he had to move to Alice Springs. The support helps him, she said, but he is very upset because he wants to come home. The whole community is "upset" that he can't come home because he is missing out on the training he needs so that the Elders can "hand over Country to him." Without this handing over of responsibility, she said, "our spirit will be gone."

For many First Nations peoples living in remote and regional areas, the NDIS gives them no choice but to move from their traditional lands. As the Disability Royal Commission commented in their hearings, the fundamental need of First Nations people to maintain links with their community and Country is not being met.

Support outside the NDIS

So far, we have looked at the situation for disabled people who have individual funding packages under the NDIS, the cohort called Tier 3.

What of those who are not NDIS participants but who still need some support? Despite continuous growth in the scheme, only a small percentage of people with disabilities – about 14 per cent, or almost 600,000 Australians – are on the NDIS, but an estimated 4.4 million Australians live with disability. This is the cohort that the NDIS calls Tier 2 – those who haven't met the criteria of "significantly reduced functioning in self-care and other areas and require significant ongoing support" or, alternatively, haven't qualified for early intervention. The NDIS was originally intended to support those without individual funding by fostering a more inclusive society and by providing Local Area Coordinators to help connect disabled people and their family to disability services within the community and within mainstream services such as hospitals and education.

In practice, however, the NDIS has not fulfilled this commitment. Due to the staffing caps, the NDIA shifted Local Area Coordinators over to become planners for individual funding packages. In any event, non-NDIS disability services were slowly and quietly disappearing. After the NDIS was introduced, a range of supports within the community and within mainstream services were neglected, provided insufficiently or depleted of funds. These include some Home and Community Care programs, local government disability services and community disability services (particularly psychosocial supports). There are also questions and buck-passing about who has responsibility for disability support in areas such as health, education, employment, transport, housing and aged care. Since the NDIS doesn't provide supports that are seen to be a government department's responsibility, it is also important to disabled people with NDIS funding that supports are available in these areas. For example, the NDIS may fund a speech pathologist for a child with a learning disability, but it won't fund a teacher's aide in the classroom, which is seen as an education department responsibility.

Research by the Melbourne Disability Institute shows that 90 per cent of disabled persons without NDIS funding who took part in the survey were unable to access the services and supports they needed. The research also indicates that much support within the community appears to have been "frozen in time," because services were not rolled over when short-term funding ended. They found that despite a great deal of information about services and supports seemingly open to people with a disability, including resources and databases designed to help people find them, this information led nowhere.

The NDIS has become such a dominant player in Australia's disability strategy that the impact can be felt if it doesn't contribute to broader inclusion. All governments have significantly increased funding for disability services in the past decade, but almost all this funding – 93 per cent – has gone to the NDIS. The states, in particular, dealt with the pressure to fund their share of the scheme by moving funding away from non-NDIS programs.

The problem, as Bruce Bonyhady often says, is that instead of a sliding scale of supports, there is now the NDIS and then a precipice. Many more people are on the NDIS than the government expected. The number of people on the scheme is growing at a higher rate than predicted, as is the average funding for each participant. Bill Shorten says it's because the NDIS has become the only lifeboat in the ocean; Bruce Bonyhady likens it to an oasis in the desert.

In particular, the number of young children entering the NDIS under the early intervention criteria has grown more than expected. A large proportion of NDIS participants have a primary diagnosis of autism – about 34 per cent overall, and 55 per cent of those under eighteen.

Once, autistic children with fewer support needs, the level 1 diagnoses, would have received support in the community or through the education system. A spokesperson from the peak autism body, Amaze, said recently that families used to have access to a wider range of autism supports, but they dried up when the NDIS was developed. As the autism researcher Andrew Whitehouse has stated, "There is evidence, for example, that practitioners started diagnosing autism in children more prematurely than they usually would, in order to help those children access support through the NDIS." This has had the opposite effect to that intended. The NDIS was supposed to get away from the medical model of disability. Access was to be based on the level of functional impairment, rather than a particular diagnosis. Focusing on each person's functional capacity allows support to be tailored to their individual needs and desires.

One of the legislative goals of the NDIS was to facilitate greater community inclusion of disabled people. The scheme would be one of a number of strategies for removing barriers in society under the broader framework of the National Disability Strategy. However, the focus on individual solutions has resulted in a neglect of broader changes. People with disabilities have been fighting for accessible public transport for a long time. We thought we were finally getting somewhere when, in 2002, Disability Transport Standards were legislated. These standards bound Australia's public transport providers to progressively modify their systems to meet minimum standards of access within twenty years. Disability advocates had spoken out against the unreasonably long timeframe, but the transport industry was powerful and a compromise was made rather than risk having no standards. The twenty-year deadline recently expired and Australia's public transport did not meet the required standards. The government says it wants to address the low participation rate of people with disabilities, particularly in employment. Yet it continues to provide a public transport system that shuts disabled people out.

Outcomes and sustainability

Reliable data on NDIS outcomes and financial sustainability is lacking. Despite quarterly reporting by the NDIA, it is difficult to assess what proportion of people on the NDIS are receiving the support they need or whether community participation is increasing. Whether the complex needs of disabled people are being met can't be measured in the same way you might measure whether something like an electricity service is working or not. Since privatisation and government withdrawal from funding or delivering services, there is no coordinated knowledge of how supports are being used. While the actuaries, the NDIA board and to some extent the Commonwealth government have authority over the scheme, the real knowledge about the scheme's operation exists at the lower and local level, among the service providers and advocates, and people with disabilities themselves.

The cost of the scheme has risen beyond what was anticipated. The NDIS was reported to have cost $35.8 billion in 2022–23, more than Medicare. Based on this rise, the government actuary has projected an increase in expenditure from 1.48 per cent of GDP in 2022–23 to 2.55 per cent in 2031–32. The actuary also projects that by 2032, the scheme will be supporting 3.3 per cent of the population, up from 2.1 per cent on 30 June 2022.

Although the projected cost of the NDIS has risen, there is no evidence of sustainability issues. One study in fact concludes that the NDIS is generating greater productivity in the economy.

Among the reasons given for the scheme's rise in cost beyond what was anticipated, the most apparent is that more people are receiving individual supports than had been expected. As noted, there are now about 600,000 people receiving individual supports rather than the original estimate of 475,000. This increase has at least partly been driven by the fact that disability supports outside the NDIS have been depleted, so that people with disabilities have to go on the NDIS or get nothing. Related to this, the number of people leaving the scheme is less than half the official forecast.

However, there are a number of reasons to question allegations of cost overruns. In 2017, the federal government announced that due to overspending there would be an NDIS funding gap of $55.7 billion over ten years. In 2019, however, they admitted to a $6.5 billion error in the NDIS forecasts and announced that the NDIS had in fact underspent. There is a continuing lack of information about the true cost of the scheme. This is part of the trend of governments letting go of responsibility for the scheme's administration.

Another, more important reason is the fact that the NDIS does not exist in a vacuum. Outcomes and financial sustainability are inextricably linked. When state or federal governments cut costs to other programs, such as support for people with disabilities in health and education, the costs of the NDIS necessarily increase. For example, in August 2023, the Victorian government cut funding for specialised teachers who work with disabled students in schools. Parents of disabled students have said this forces them to apply for private therapists under the NDIS at four times the cost. At the same time, when NDIS supports are inadequate or non-existent, the costs fall heavily on other parts of the system. For example, because of a lack of at-home support, in 2022 NDIS participants remained in hospital for an average of 160 days after they were medically fit to be discharged. Reforms that expedited the availability of at-home supports are estimated to have saved the health system $550 million.

Similarly, when government washes its hands of responsibility, leaving market mechanisms to deliver services, or fail to deliver them, this leads to more expensive services. When broader issues such as making society and the built environment accessible are neglected, this leads to individuals needing more individual support. When government spends money on costly NDIS disputes in the AAT and Federal Court, this also increases the cost of the scheme. When governments lose expertise in scheme administration, or adopt a "steer, not row" approach with little supervision of the service providers' operations, this leads to an increase in fraud, and therefore scheme costs. How the NDIS operates has implications for the cost of mainstream services such as health and education — and, conversely, how mainstream services operate has implications for the NDIS and its cost.

It is always possible to dispute figures and projections from economists. These are only putting dollar figures on more intangible and difficult-to-measure qualities. Economic modelling is notoriously abstruse and sometimes inhuman in its assumptions about the dollar value of human lives – a strange and paradoxical way of measuring something designed to restore human dignity to lives which might otherwise be lived without it. However, for the survival and sustainability of the NDIS, it will always be important that its costs are predictable for governments and the public. It is crucially important that NDIS money is spent effectively, not on unnecessary or shoddy "therapies" which service providers charge for, but which do not actually benefit the disabled person. Supported Independent Living services also urgently need review, given that about $10 billion goes into these services each year, to support about 30,000 people to live independently, but a royal commission has heard significant abuse and neglect occurs in these settings. Fraud is a continuing problem for the NDIS model, and clearly needs to be reined in – but just as importantly, unethical practices short of fraud need to be stopped – in particular, people being overcharged for services or pressured into spending money on services they do not need. And most importantly, we need to reform and improve the services that sit around the NDIS, increasing community and mainstream supports so that people can access other services without needing to apply for NDIS funding.

Reports of "cost blow-outs" also lose sight of the contribution NDIS spending makes to the economy. The original insurance approach was based on this assumption – that eventually the scheme would not only pay for itself but would also generate revenue and productivity through increased employment of support workers, carers and people with disabilities. To some extent, these original aims have not been realised. The low employment rates of disabled persons in Australia have remained about the same, between 52 per cent and 55 per cent between 1993 and 2019 – with, if anything, a slight drop from the high of 54.9 per cent in 1993. More family carers of disabled persons, however, have been able to return to work.

Although the projected cost of the NDIS has risen, there is no evidence of sustainability issues. According to one study, the NDIS employs over 270,000 people, and contributes indirectly to the employment of tens of thousands more. The study concludes that the NDIS is generating greater productivity in the economy, arguing that the "multiplier effect" of the scheme is in the range of 2.25, meaning that its economic contribution in 2020–21 was about $52.4 billion.

I am flying to Byron Bay for some writers' festival events, which I'm looking forward to. From Melbourne to Ballina, the closest airport, is a two-hour direct flight. But the airline has refused to take me unless I travel with a carer. Its policy is to refuse assistance to disabled people who can't transfer to the aeroplane seat independently. I am meeting a support worker in Byron who will help me during my stay. I didn't want to arrange an additional support worker just to fly up with me and return by themselves. It would have cost the NDIS about fourteen hours of the support worker's time, and it would have cost me their return ticket. I wanted to make a disability discrimination complaint against the airline for its unreasonable refusal to provide the necessary support, but there was no time.

There was only one airline I could find, a much more expensive one, that allowed disabled people needing help to travel without a carer. It provides the "eagle hoist." This nifty piece of equipment lifts you out of the wheelchair, travels down the narrow cabin aisle and lowers you to your seat. But the airline did not offer a direct flight. It offered a three-hour journey, including a stop for a connecting flight in Sydney. I calculated that even were the plane delayed for an hour, I would be able to hold off going to the toilet until I reached my destination. Chances were it would work out. Still, I was anxious for days before the travel because I worried about missing the connecting flight and what I would do if I needed to go to the toilet and couldn't.

To prepare for the journey, I ate and drank nothing that morning. I knew it was unhealthy, but sometimes there was little choice. Some of my friends who also used electric wheelchairs have kidney stones from regularly dehydrating themselves when they go out. Even if you find a designated accessible public toilet, you may not be able to use it because it's being used as a storage room, or wasn't actually built to disability access standards.

Going through security at Melbourne airport, I asked the officer if he could help lift the bag off the back of my wheelchair onto the screening table. "Where's your carer?" he asked. I told him I was travelling alone. "You should have a carer to help you with that," he said. I was taken aback; in the past, airport staff had always helped. The woman behind me in the queue muttered, "Unbelievable," and lifted my bag onto the belt. I could have kissed her.

Next, I met the wheelchair assistance officer at the boarding gate, and he asked me where my carer was. And similarly, on the plane, the flight attendant asked, "Who's assisting you?" In other services as well, since the NDIS, I had noticed this expectation that the disabled person should bring their own support. A hospital administrator making an appointment asked me to make sure that I brought a support worker if I needed assistance to get onto the testing table, whereas in the past the hospital staff always provided that help. My disabled friends have also remarked on this trend. One of them told me his supermarket had stopped helping him collect items and insisted he have a carer to do that.

I arrive at Sydney airport only to find that the connecting flight has been cancelled and the next one is four hours later. My heart starts pumping faster. I ask the airline assistant who is pushing me in an aircraft wheelchair if he can bring my electric wheelchair to me. He makes a call, then tells me that all the luggage needs to stay on the plane.

"My wheelchair is not luggage," I cry out. "I can't move without my wheelchair." The chair I am strapped into is what the airline uses to fit between the aisles in the aeroplane. It's a thin wedge of a chair that is hard for me to balance on and you can't push it yourself. He parks me on a square of carpet with a wheelchair symbol on it some distance from the service desk and the customer seating area. He tells me he'll let them know at the service desk that I want my wheelchair. "Can you take me over so I can speak with them myself?" I ask, but he has already walked off.

It's an hour later. They have finally agreed to bring out my electric wheelchair but it has still not arrived. It's a new person at the service desk now and I call out to get her attention. She is busy with customers and doesn't hear. I call out to passengers passing by but they don't look my way. I am tired and anxious and don't know how I'm going to manage on my own until the next flight. The busy people bustle past and I feel anxious and abandoned, like detritus.

Why didn't I just bring a support worker with me! I'm bitterly regretting it now, but I know it isn't just the expense to the NDIS that made me decide to travel solo. It has more to do with protest. I don't want the NDIS to take the focus off the need for society to be more inclusive. The NDIS has helped to minimise the individual effects of my condition, but it has not helped make society more accessible. Strengthening individual support for some should not deflect from making structural change in society – but this is what has happened.

I could go around all day with a support worker and be safe and supported. And I could continually scout ahead to locate the limited places that are accessible and go only there. But I don't want to be confined to my own little lifeboat. I want my community to be open to all and inclusive. I want to get bogged at a beach in my wheelchair and know people will help. I want to push into a crowded, heaving mosh pit and join the other dancers.

These hopes seem so lofty now when I see what the NDIS has become. Many would be relieved just to be able to scramble onto the NDIS lifeboat. But we mustn't forget the three main things we asked for. First, disabled people wanted the scheme to operate as a right or an entitlement; second, disabled people should have "choice and control" to ensure that the support provided matches their needs and goals; and third, the support should enable them to participate in the life of the community. The NDIS has not yet delivered on these. In the words of Bill Shorten, the current responsible minister, who recently returned to government after nine years of Coalition rule, the scheme "has lost its way."

For all of the stated goals, and the policies we fought for to ensure that the NDIS would reflect a human rights approach and the social model of disability, it is the individual model of disability that the designers of the NDIS reverted to in its implementation. They conceived of disability as something that can be fixed by empowering the individual as a consumer. Once again, the burden is on the individual to fight for access rather than society taking responsibility for removing the barriers.

The scheme implementers cast aside the voice and leadership of disabled people and created an NDIS that is difficult to access; employs a dysfunctional market approach; and neglects broader community inclusion. Without both disability supports and the removal of society's barriers, you can't have increased participation.

In practice, the scheme offers only individual funding for disability support and equipment to those with disabilities deemed to be the most significant. They must be able to attract supports which the market chooses, and have the capacity (themselves or through advocates) to convert that funding to the support they need. This wasn't what the architects of the scheme intended. It was not intended to be so individualised, narrow and inequitable. It was supposed to make broad social changes and help all people with disabilities. It was especially not supposed to be harmful to those most isolated and in need of assistance. The story of Anne-Marie Smith is difficult to think about.

Anne-Marie Smith had cerebral palsy. She lived in a well-to-do Adelaide suburb with her parents. Her life was good, according to a friend's account, until her last surviving parent died around 2010. Then she gradually became more isolated. Old photos show Anne-Marie with decorative clips in her shiny hair sitting in a wheelchair playing with her beloved dogs. Under the old disability care system, a case manager employed by the South Australian government was responsible for ensuring Anne-Marie received the services she needed.

In 2018, Anne-Marie was registered with the NDIS to receive care for six hours a day, seven days a week, from the provider Integrity Care. In April 2020, at the age of fifty-four, Anne-Marie died a terrible and degrading death from extreme neglect. The sole support worker had left Anne-Marie confined to the same woven cane chair in the lounge room for over a year. Anne-Marie died from septic shock, organ failure, infected pressure sores and malnutrition.

In 2017, preparing for Anne-Marie's transition to the NDIS, the SA officer provided a transfer document to the NDIA that explained that Anne-Marie had a deteriorating condition and difficulties understanding complex matters. The transfer document stated the NDIA planner was required to meet with Anne-Marie in person and also allow her to have a friend there to support her. The NDIA ignored this requirement. For Anne-Marie's first plan, an NDIA planner merely called her over the phone in the presence of her abusive support worker. At Anne-Marie's second annual plan, the NDIA once again failed to meet in person with Anne-Marie. Once again, they spoke over the phone with the abusive support worker.

The support worker is now in prison for manslaughter and the service provider has been banned. But what of the NDIA's responsibility? The NDIA ignored the request for a face-to-face meeting and a support friend and provided no equivalent of the previous case manager to oversee and be responsible for Anne-Marie's care. And what of the governments and the NDIA board that set up this market approach which showed no care?

In the Royal Commission inquiry relating to Ms Smith's death, Martin Hoffman, the former CEO of the NDIA, in his statement on issues of responsibility, said that the NDIS "operates on the presumption that all people with disability have the capacity to make decisions and exercise choice and control." The Royal Commission members commented that Hoffman's view does not respond to the concern "that some people with disability are in a position of heightened risk and that the bodies concerned with the services and supports they receive should take additional steps to safeguard them."

Anne-Marie's suffering and degradation shocked the community. It has also frightened and disturbed disabled people, for whom her situation has become symbolic of an uncaring system. In neglecting to ensure that any safeguards were in place, the NDIS helped to create the defencelessness and the isolation that allowed the abuse to occur. The response by the former CEO of the NDIA is chilling. He has ignored reality and dehumanised Anne-Marie. The CEO may be in breach of the NDIS laws that require the

CEO to act in compliance with the principle that "People with disability will be supported in their dealings and communications with the NDIA so that their capacity to exercise choice and control is maximised." The CEO has confused Anne-Marie's right to self-determination, or capacity, with the ability to act on her own without any support. Anne-Marie's right to self-determination is only guaranteed by receiving the support she needs to exercise that right.

The NDIS is repeatedly described as a financial burden, a cause of cost blow-outs, and users of the NDIS have been portrayed as either scammers or victims. Disability is portrayed as a burden to be paid for by the "productive" members of society. Political opponents scaremonger about the cost of the scheme, although they themselves have amplified these by cutting short-term costs so the scheme can't flourish, neglecting disability supports outside the NDIS, and implementing a market model that's not fit for purpose. And as the Productivity Commission and the actuaries repeat, "the ultimate cap – and test of financial sustainability – is taxpayers' continuing willingness to pay for it." We find ourselves fearful.

And suddenly I am back alone in class with my big book of fairytales while the other children play. Only as an adult did I learn that these seductive tales were also lessons designed to keep the poor in their place. No getting above your station, Little Mermaid! Be grateful for what you have, or you'll end up like the fisherman and his wife.

A poor fisherman lives with his wife in a filthy shack by the sea. One day the fisherman catches a flounder, who claims to be able to grant wishes and begs to be set free. The fisherman kindly releases it. When his wife hears the story, she says he ought to have had the fish grant him a wish. She insists that he go back and ask the flounder to grant her wish for a nice house. The fisherman goes back to the sea and the flounder grants his wish and he returns home to a pretty little cottage. But soon the cottage is too small and his wife is not satisfied and sends the fisherman back to the flounder in the sea to ask for a palace. The flounder grants his wish. But still the wife is not satisfied, and she asks for more. Each time the fisherman goes out to ask for more, the sea is darker and wilder, until finally he goes out to sea amid thunder and lightning and black waves as high as church towers. When the fisherman makes his wish, the flounder says, "Go home. She is sitting in her filthy shack again."

The tide is turning. In October 2022, Minister Shorten announced a review of the NDIS, looking at design, operations and sustainability, as well as ways to make the market and workforce more sustainable and responsive. The Independent Review of the National Disability Insurance Scheme is co-chaired by Bruce Bonyhady. It is due to make its recommendations to disability ministers in a final report in October 2023. Around the same time, a major inquiry that started in 2019, the Royal Commission into Violence, Abuse, Neglect and Exploitation of People with Disability, will be reporting.

There have been over a dozen reviews of the NDIS since its commencement, but the Independent Review is different. We have learnt from the mistakes of the past ten years and this review has been co-designed with disabled people. With this one comes a rallying cry to bring back the spirit and campaigning voice that brought the NDIS into being.

With the return of the Labor government, the chair of the NDIA board is now a disabled person, Kurt Fearnley, and half of the board members are people with lived experience of disability. An extra $720 million has been committed to build the capacity of the NDIA.

Shorten has also focused on clearing a large backlog of Administrative Appeals Tribunal disputes, mainly comprising reviews of NDIA decisions to refuse supports or access to the scheme, and on reducing delays that saw NDIS participants languishing in hospitals for months waiting for disability supports to become available.

As for cost overruns, Shorten has called on the states to honour their responsibilities to fund disability services within the community so that the NDIS isn't "the only lifeboat in the ocean" and to target unscrupulous service providers price-gouging or defrauding the scheme.

The proof of a commitment to the original goals of the NDIS will be whether the government takes responsibility for providing effective and equitable disability supports without hiding behind a "leave it to the market" approach and ensures that the broader changes to make society more inclusive are not neglected.

The political scientist Mark Considine, who has researched the impact of the market system on the NDIS, says that improvements can be made that are not expensive and will likely save money over time. The scheme needs to be made more community-based, and to rely on shared expertise within the existing services to find the best ways of doing things. We need to define what service providers are supposed to do, and make sure these meet the needs of disabled people, now and in the future. Service models should be transparent, so that information and innovation can be shared, and employees trained more easily. Public service providers need to be brought back into delivering services. The public service can't improve a service if its staff don't have experience working with it, and the public service should be a "provider of last resort." Importantly, he argues for a shift from "choice to voice," which would mean that instead of service providers competing to deliver the same service, they specialise in a way that genuinely meets community needs, wherever people are. "Voice" means that disabled people must be listened to, their experience valued – for example, by requiring that agencies include disabled people on their boards.

But the real question is how the reforms of the review will be implemented. How do we ensure that they respond to people's different capabilities, needs and context? How do we make sure the same mistakes aren't made again?

It is too simplistic to blame all the mistakes on the approach of the Coalition government that was responsible for the first nine years of implementation. Many Western governments, both labour and conservative, have tried to use the market to deliver social change and often ignored the raft of economic literature on why markets fail. The market approach has been the federal government's approach to public services for decades, so in some ways the reliance on the market to deliver the NDIS was just "business as usual."

Yet it is still difficult to reconcile that the government would have supported the creation of a multi-billion-dollar scheme aimed at improving the lives of disabled persons and at the same time set it up so that many of them couldn't actually use the scheme or would be put at risk by it. Surely they could not have genuinely expected every NDIS participant to be the rational autonomous person able to contract for and attract services? And in what alternate universe would a government assume that under a market model, services would be readily available for every participant to choose, even when participants lived in remote areas or required very specialised care?

I had an interesting conversation with Bruce Bonyhady three years ago about whether a human rights approach had been given sufficient priority in the design of the NDIS. "As Adam Smith said, people are both self-regarding and other-regarding or altruistic," Bruce noted. "Insurance appeals to people's self-interest in a way that human rights don't. Some people see human rights as something that a minority goes on about too loudly and so an emphasis on human rights might have risked rejection of the NDIS." I understand that the NDIS may not have received bipartisan support without the promised financial sustainability and investment framing of an insurance approach. That support was also needed to survive possible changes of government during the ten years it would take to build an institution as large as the NDIS. But it becomes self-defeating if we have to underplay the importance of human rights in order to pander to biases or governments' preoccupation with wealth maximisation.

When I look at the way people respond to disability, I see this as influenced more by how they understand disability than by whether they are altruistic. We live in a society still shaped by a history of denying the humanity of disabled persons, of seeing the person's condition as the problem and not recognising how disadvantage is caused and how to respond to these realities.

How people understand disability transforms how they respond to it. When they saw us as cursed or contaminated, they banished us, euthanised us or left us on the streets to perish. When they saw us as requiring protection, they institutionalised us. When they saw us as defective and in need of a cure, we were hospitalised and medicalised. When they saw us as tragic, they treated us as objects of charity. Now the NDIS, still influenced by an individual or medical model of disability, has given us a new identity: consumer.

Recognition that people with disabilities are equal is vital. If it was accepted that we are equal and capable of making significant contributions, society at large would be more willing to take concrete steps to include us. The NDIS needs to lead cultural change rather than replicate discriminatory structures. The scheme in its goals and design was in many ways indeed transformative, but the cultural change needed to deliver the scheme has not been given priority and we have fallen into the old ruts – an over-reliance on market solutions, people without lived experience making the rules on what people with disabilities need, representation of people with disabilities as an economic burden, an inability to respond to the structural causes of disadvantage. People in subordinated positions have access to knowledge and understanding about systems of power that the advantaged do not have, and a system like the NDIS can't work effectively if it does not draw on this knowledge.

The Disability Rights Convention approach provides four dimensions to ensure that reforms advance the human rights of disabled persons. The first dimension concerns taking steps to redress the disadvantage attached to living with a disability. This involves responding to people's different capabilities, needs and context. To have real choice and control means having the necessary supports to be able to exercise this choice and control. The second dimension of the framework requires recognising individual dignity and redressing stigma, stereotyping and prejudice. The third dimension calls for participation and inclusion in society. In particular, disabled persons must be involved at every level of decision-making in matters concerning them. Finally, the fourth dimension concerns the need for structural change to accommodate difference and remove barriers that prevent inclusion.

Unless you change how people think about things, you're not really going to change their actions or responses. As the philosopher Nancy Fraser has said, "To be misrecognized ... is not simply to be thought ill of, looked down upon or devalued in others' attitudes, beliefs or representations. It is rather to be denied the status of a full partner in social interaction, as a consequence of institutionalized patterns of cultural value that constitute one as comparatively unworthy of respect or esteem." Nelson Mandela put it more trenchantly: "To deny people their human rights is to challenge their very humanity."

Acknowledging the vulnerability of our bodies is also important, because it is what joins us as humans. Every person will experience bodily limitation, from being wholly dependent as a baby through to injury, mental health days, illness and ageing. In fact, it is through acceptance of our universal condition of vulnerability that the attitudes in our society which cause segregation are most likely to be changed. Disability needs to be seen as part of the normal variation of life, such that the measures to make society inclusive are also normal. In this way, steps to remove barriers in society and to provide disability supports are simple responses to a realistic conception of who humans are, rather than a burden imposed on others.

If buildings and systems are designed and built using the principles of universal design, they will not only benefit people with disabilities, but also be more responsive to the needs of all people, including children, the aged and those with temporary impairments.

Warm-water pools, or what were once called hydrotherapy pools, are places where I can meet and bump up against the whole of humanity. Frida and I started going together to such a pool when we were housemates. She always had a sense of occasion and bought us both rubber floral swim caps so we could look the part when – as she tried to coax me to – we did synchronised swimming in the pool. Frida would try to get others in the pool to join in the moves as well, and most people loved her goofy and exaggerated attempts at gracefulness. Now I go to my local warm-water pool twice a week. In the water my body is unanchored, and every part of me becomes warm and alive. I'm able to go there because the facilities are accessible and because the NDIS funds a support worker to help me into the pool.

There is a woman I see there who reminds me of Frida. She comes at the busiest times, she tells me she likes it that way, and she will position herself just where people enter and exit the pool for maximum contact.

She smiles and waves and talks with the swimmers, the parents and their children there for swim class and everybody in between. She, too, like Frida did, will try to teach them some moves, but hers are not synchronised swimming, hers are fitness exercises. She tries to teach me too, and I've learnt that she is usually isolated and the pool is where she comes to be with people. One or two of the swimmers have complained about her unorthodox behaviour to the pool management, but they're good there at the pool I go to and they have supported her.

I love it too, that coming up close to everybody. I need a particular depth and to hold onto a wall rail to do my exercises. Others also covet that spot. I negotiate with older people for the spot, and small children just clamber over and around me. Once a young man who looked like a Greek god stood in my spot and we chatted and I found out he had an injury. "Do you know who you were speaking to?" a regular at the pool came up to say to me when he left. "The Bont." I don't know anything about football, but I made sure I remembered the name so I could tell my son, who is footy-mad.

Accepting the reality of our bodies and human vulnerability can create new ways of seeing and being in the world that will enrich our lives. Why, for instance, is grace and the look of effortlessness beautiful, but the sight of struggle not?

The NDIS is a powerful establishment on which we can build. At its heart is the Australian ideal of the fair go. The legislation is underpinned by this goal. If we stay true to it, the structures and the attitudes that disadvantage people with disabilities can be transformed. The mistakes in the implementation of the NDIS can be righted. The first step to bringing the NDIS back on course is to be aware of the deeply entrenched biases that lead people to act in ways that disregard the dignity and equal value of disabled people.

When I was young, I spent a lot of time fearing a future where my disability would progress to an intolerable stage. I imagined that point would be when I was dependent on help to get out of bed, go to the toilet, shower and dress myself. I'm at that point now. Each time I lose more of my physical strength, first I object, I grieve, and then, like most people do, I adapt. I have no less love, interests and passion in my life. The sun is still marvellous, and the sky blue. Like everyone else, I have my own goals, successes and struggles. Life is normal.

At least it feels normal, until I see people's eyes on me and feel their pity, their admiration that I go on living, their horror, or their thankfulness that they are not me. The thing that they want to deny is that they are me. This stops empathy and makes it easy for people to treat us with less dignity than they would like for themselves. Dependency or vulnerability is inherent to our humanity. All humans are born and usually die dependent, and we live with the ever-present possibility of injury or disability.

When I was eighteen, I was nearly overwhelmed by the anxiety of becoming increasingly disabled and being dependent and without supports. This fear drove me to throw myself into a situation where I was powerless. I travelled in Europe and Africa alone, without any support. I was spurred on to experience everything, not miss out, *never miss out*, no matter how hard it was.

Paradoxically, by experiencing my own helplessness, I was able to discover my inherent worth and power. I remember Kamanja, a man I met in Kenya. He was one of many people who came my way and helped me through, who pushed me in my wheelchair and carried me when I was at a low ebb and battered. I started to thank him. He held out his hand for me to stop. "I help you because you need help," he said.

SOURCES

Thanks to my editor Chris Feik for trusting me with this essay. I didn't know how to meld the personal and the institutional in one essay until he said write it like a novel. Thanks also to my excellent associate editor Kirstie Innes-Will. I am grateful for the insights from my PhD supervisors Beth Gaze, Bernadette McSherry and Eddie Paterson. Thanks to Stephen Gray for the generous help, as well as to Amy Husband, Bruce Bonyhady, Maria Lovison, Jeanette Lee, Mark Lee-Gray, Ana Cristina Sandoval, Brendan O'Reilly, Kay Wilson, Betty Choi and the kind shop owner.

Many disability activists use the term "disabled people" to emphasise that it is the barriers in society that are disabling, and distinguish this from the term "impairment", which describes their biological conditions. In Australia, most institutions use the term "people with disability" in keeping with the Disability Rights Convention definition that disability results from the inter-action between persons with impairments and attitudinal and environmental barriers. I tend to use both terms interchangeably.

Small portions of the conclusion of this essay were previously published in "The Art of Dependency", The Monthly, August 2017.

9   "The scheme to be established" etc.: Julia Gillard, House of Representatives: National Disability Insurance Scheme Bill 2012, Second Reading Speech, 29 November 2012.

14   "wrong-way": Damian Griffis, First Submission to the Productivity Commission Inquiry into Disability Care and Support, First Peoples Disability Network (Australia), Submission 542, August 2010.

14   "less eligibility": Paul Ramcharan, "Understanding the NDIS: A history of disability welfare from 'deserving poor' to consumers in control", The Conversation, 6 July 2016.

16   The UN's Disability Rights Convention: UN General Assembly, Convention on the Rights of Persons with Disabilities: resolution / adopted by the General Assembly, 24 January 2007, A/RES/61/106, available at: www.refworld.org/docid/45f973632.html, accessed 13 August 2023.

16   unprecedented for any previous human rights convention: Phillip French and Rosemary Kayess, "Out of darkness into light? Introducing the Convention on the Rights of Persons with Disabilities", *Human Rights Law Review*, vol. 8, no. 1, 2008, pp. 1, 3–4.

16   It is not enough to have rights: "This idea that the Convention would not create new rights, but adapt existing rights to secure their equal enjoyment by persons with disabilities, became an omnipresent theme during its drafting." Oddný Mjöll Arnardóttir and Gerard Quinn (eds), *The UN Convention on the Rights of Persons with Disabilities: European and Scandinavian perspectives*, Martinus Nijhoff Publishers, 2009, p. 44.

16   Policies should: Sandra Fredman, "Disability equality: A challenge to the existing anti-discrimination paradigm?", *Disability and Equality Law*, Ashgate Publishing, 2013, p. 123.

20   Australia ranked lowest for the relative income of people with disabilities: Organisation for Economic Co-operation and Development, *Sickness, Disability and Work: Keeping on track in the economic downturn*, Background Paper, 2009.

20   They faced barriers: See, generally, the findings of consultations with people with disabilities in National People with Disabilities and Carers Council, *Shut Out: The experience of people with disabilities and their families in Australia*, Consultation Report, Commonwealth of Australia, 2012; Data from VicHealth, Disability and Health Inequalities in Australia, Research Summary, 22 August 2012.

22   about 4.8 million people: Luke Buckmaster and Shannon Clark, "The National Disability Insurance Scheme: A chronology", Parliamentary Library, 13 July 2018, www.aph.gov.au/About_Parliament/Parliamentary_Departments/Parliamentary_ Library/pubs/rp/rp1819/Chronologies/NDIS, accessed 9 August 2023.

22   Roughly 90 per cent of this cohort: Productivity Commission, *Disability Care and Support: Overview and recommendations*, Inquiry Report No. 54, Australian Government, vol. I, 31 July 2011, p. 160; Elizabeth Wright, Celina Edmonds and Evan Young, "Concern millions of Australians with disability not on the NDIS have been 'Forgotten'", ABC News (online), 18 May 2022.

22   for whom early intervention: Productivity Commission, *Disability Care and Support*, vol. 1, p. 26.

22   around 475,000 people: This figure was originally 411,000. It was increased to 475,000 to reflect the acceptance of people with mental illness under the scheme: Productivity Commission, *Disability Care and Support*, vol. I, pp. i–ix.

24   "mainstream services": Productivity Commission, *Disability Care and Support*, vol. 1, pp. 13–14. Also, NDIS Tier 2 would ensure that all people with disability, whether or not they had an individual NDIS plan, would "benefit from a more inclusive, accessible and connected Australia."

24   risk insurance: "Rhonda Galbally and Bruce Bonyhady on the birth of the NDIS", *Change Agents* (podcast), *The Conversation*, 10 August 2016.

24   "Governments plan for expenditures", "investments": Luke Buckmaster, "The National Disability Insurance Scheme: A quick guide", Parliament of Australia website, 3 March 2017, www.aph.gov.au/About_Parliament/Parliamentary_Departments/ Parliamentary_Library/pubs/rp/rp1617/Quick_Guides/NDIS, accessed 9 August 2023.

25   would outweigh the costs: Productivity Commission, *Disability Care and Support*, n. 9, pp. 55–6.

26   "It will change": Julia Gillard, Parliamentary Debates, House of Representatives, 29 November 2012, 13877–8.

27   Almost 600,000 people: "At 31 December 2022, 573,342 participants had an NDIS plan, and 20,477 participants entered the Scheme during the quarter," NDIA, *NDIS Quarterly Report to Disability Ministers: Q2 2022–23*, 31 December 2022, p. 17.

27   National Disability Insurance Agency (NDIA), NDIA Board, Ministerial Council: *NDIS Act 2013* (Cwlth): s118, s124, s12.

28   any scheme overspend: Helen Dickinson and Dennis Petrie, "The Budget sounded warnings of an NDIS blowout but also set aside funds to curb costs and boost productivity", *The Conversation*, 28 October 2022.

28   "to poorer outcomes", "especially early in the scheme's life": Productivity Commission, *National Disability Insurance Scheme (NDIS) Costs*, Productivity Commission Study Report, October 2017.

28   lacks even the fundamental elements of contemporary customer service: D. Winkler, M. Brown, K. D'Cruz, S. Oliver and P. Mulherin, *Getting the NDIS Back on Track: A survey of people with disability*, Summer Foundation, 2022.

30   automated decision-making process: Georgia van Toorn, Jackie Leach Scully and Karen Soldatic, "NDIS plans rely on algorithms to judge need – the upcoming review should change that", *The Conversation*, 27 October 2022.

30   swivel car seat: *Young and National Disability Insurance Agency* [2017] AATA 407.

30   all-terrain four-wheel-drive wheelchair: *Munday and National Disability Insurance Agency* [2018] AATA 355.

31   purchase of a new orthotic attachment: *Paviiupillai and NDIA* (2018) AATA 4641.

32   complex care planner: Complex planners can work more collaboratively with support coordinators than regular planners and are generally the main point of contact within the NDIA for the participant and their supports. Team DSC, "Exceptionally complex support needs program", Team DSC website, 9 November 2020, teamdsc.com.au/resources/exceptionally-complex-support-needs-program, accessed 9 August 2023.

33   More reports were emerging: Victoria Legal Aid and the Office of Public Advocate documented the stories of about twenty clients with complex needs in Victoria

who experienced avoidable imprisonment, homelessness and/or serious risks to their health and wellbeing because of changes brought by the NDIS.

33 "business risk": Victoria Legal Aid, Submission to the Federal Joint Standing Committee on National Disability Insurance Scheme Costs, 14 July 2017.

33 withdrawn support: Victoria Legal Aid, *Ten Stories of NDIS "Thin Markets": Reforming the NDIS to meet people's needs*, 2019; Office of the Public Advocate, *The Illusion of Choice and Control*, 2018.

34 "intermediary" services: Padraic Fleming, Sinead McGilloway and Steve Thomas, "Individualised funding: A realist analysis to identify the causal factors that facilitate positive outcomes", *Disabilities*, vol. 1, no. 1, 2021, pp. 47–57; Padraic Fleming et al., "Individualized funding options to improve health and social care outcomes for people with a disability: A mixed methods systematic review", *Campbell Systematic Reviews*, vol. 15, no. 1–2, June 2019.

34 most of this responsibility has fallen to the individual: Joint Standing Committee on the National Disability Insurance Scheme, *Joint Committee Market Readiness*, Parliament of Australia, 20 September 2018, pp. 71–5; Gemma Carey, Eleanor Malbon and James Blackwell, "Administering inequality? The National Disability Insurance Scheme and administrative burdens on individuals", *Australian Journal of Public Administration*, vol. 80, no. 4, 2021, p. 155.

34 "steer, not row", "Central": NDIA, *Towards an Ordinary Life*, NDIS Annual Report 2015–16, 2016, p. 18.

34 "People with disabilities": NDIS, *NDIS Market Approach: Statement of opportunity and intent*, November 2016, p. 14.

38 twenty-two minutes ... much more likely to be seen as a non-person when disengaged: Chris Bigby, Director, "What Does Best Practice Look Like?" presentation given at DSC NDIS conference 2 June 2023.

39 fundamental need of First Nations people: Disability Royal Commission, Transcript Day 1, Public Hearing 25, Alice Springs, p. 6.

40 particularly psychosocial supports: One example of a community service is the mental health program Partners in Recovery, which had its funding transferred to the NDIS: Theresa Williams and Geoffrey Smith, "Mental health and the NDIS: Making it work for people with psychosocial disability", in Mhairi Cowden and Claire McCullagh, *The National Disability Insurance Scheme: An Australian public policy experiment*, Palgrave MacMillan, 2021, p. 172.

40 questions and buck-passing: The Victorian Education department recently cut the number of visiting disability specialist teachers from 117 to thirty-two.

40 "frozen in time": Sue Olney, Amber Mills and Liam Fallon, "The Tier 2 tipping point: Access to support for working-age Australians with disability without individual NDIS funding" (executive summary), Melbourne Disability Institute, University of Melbourne, 2022, p. 8.

40   93 per cent: NDIS Review, *What We Have Heard: Moving from defining problems to designing solutions to build a better NDIS*, Australian Government, June 2023, p. 8: funding for disability services rose from $8.2 billion in 2012–13 to $31.3 billion in 2021–22.

40   moving funding away: Mark Considine, *The Careless State: Reforming Australia's social services*, Melbourne University Press, 2022, pp. 122–3. This gravitational shift away from non-NDIS services was accelerated by funding issues. The Productivity Commission had originally assumed that there would continue to be non-NDIS programs available to meet the needs of people with disabilities who did not qualify or did not choose to be on the NDIS. For this to occur, the states would have to have continued to allocate significant funds to non-NDIS services. However, the Commonwealth was under political pressure to deliver a budget surplus after the global financial crisis. This meant they put additional pressure on the states to fund their share of the NDIS. The states dealt with this pressure by moving funding away from non-NDIS programs, into the NDIS.

41   primary diagnosis of autism: NDIS Quarterly Report to disability ministers, 30 June 2022, p. 32; see also NDIS Autism Summary, September 2022, at https://data.NDIS.gov.au/reports-and-analyses/participant-dashboards/autism; and Samra Alispahic and Andrew Whitehouse, "An autism minister may boost support and coordination. But governments that follow South Australia's lead should be cautious", *The Conversation*, 18 August 2022.

41   spokesperson from the peak autism body, Amaze: Jim Mullan, chief executive, Amaze, quoted in Natassia Chrysanthos, "Sharp rise: More than 8 per cent of young school children now on NDIS", *The Age*, 19 May 2023.

41   "There is evidence": Andrew Whitehouse, "Should ADHD be in the NDIS? Yes, but eligibility for disability supports should depend on the person not the diagnosis", *The Conversation*, 29 September 2022. See also Stephanie Dalzell and Michael McKinnon, "Doctors say they cut corners to help 'forgotten children' access NDIS funding", ABC News, 14 February 2020.

42   the real knowledge about the scheme's operation: Gemma Carey, Eleanor Malbon and James Blackwell, "Administering inequality? The National Disability Insurance Scheme and administrative burdens on individuals", *Australian Journal of Public Administration*, vol. 80, no. 4, 2021, p. 157.

42   federal government announced: Andrew Charlton, "The fatal flaw in the NDIS: It cries wolf but has no shepherd to control its spending", *The Sydney Morning Herald*, 9 July 2021.

43   Victorian government cut funding: Robyn Grace, "Vulnerable children to lose classroom support in big cut to specialised teachers", *The Age*, 2 August 2023.

43   saved the health system $550 million: Helen Dickinson, "The NDIS is set for a reboot but we also need to reform disability services outside the scheme", *The Conversation*, 19 April 2023.

44   notoriously abstruse and sometimes inhuman: Richard Denniss, "Spreadsheets of power: How economic modelling is used to circumvent democracy and shut down debate", *The Monthly*, April 2015.

44   significant abuse and neglect occurs in these settings: NDIS Review, *What We Have Heard: Moving from defining problems to designing solutions to build a better NDIS*, Australian Government, June 2023, p. 22.

44   overcharged for services or pressured into spending money on services they do not need: Dickinson, "The NDIS is set for a reboot".

44   reform and improve the services that sit around the NDIS: Dickinson, "The NDIS is set for a reboot".

44   slight drop from the high of 54.9 per cent in 1993: The labour force participation rates of people with disability were at 54.9 per cent in 1993, compared with 52.8 per cent in 2012, according to the Australian Bureau of Statistics, "4433.0.55.006 – Disability and Labour Force Participation, 2012", ABS website 5 February 2015, www.abs.gov.au/ausstats/abs@.nsf/mf/4433.0.55.006, accessed 9 August 2023. The labour force participation rate remained stable at 53.4 per cent between 2015 to 2019: Australian Bureau of Statistics, "Disability, Ageing and Carers, Australia: Summary of Findings", ABS website, 24 October 2019, www.abs.gov.au/statistics/health/disability/disability-ageing-and-carers-australia-summary-findings/latest-release, accessed 9 August 2023. According to the NDIA, 20.2 per cent of the participants noted they had a job, while 31.3 per cent said they were unemployed but wanted a job: NDIA, *Employment Outcomes for NDIS Participants*, 31 December 2020, p. 23.

45   NDIS employs over 270,000 people: Michael D'Rosario and Matt Lloyd-Cape, *False Economy: The economic benefits of the National Disability Insurance Scheme and the consequences of government cost-cutting*, Per Capita, 3 November 2021, p. 3.

45   economic contribution in 2020–21 was about $52.4 billion: D'Rosario and Lloyd-Cape, *False Economy*, Executive Summary, p. 2.

50   "operates on the presumption": Alan Robertson SC, "Independent review of the adequacy of the regulation of the supports and services provided to Ms Ann-Marie Smith, an NDIS participant, who died on 6 April 2020", Exhibit 14-202, "Statement of Martin Hoffman", 20 May 2021, at [76].

50   "that some people": Disability Royal Commission, *Public Hearing 14: Preventing and*

responding to violence, abuse, neglect and exploitation in disability services (South Australia), para. 244, p. 77.

51 Anne-Marie's right to self-determination is only guaranteed by receiving the support she needs to exercise that right: The Disability Rights Convention also strongly articulates this principle by obliging states to provide access to the supports needed that will help the person make their own decisions.

51 "the ultimate cap": Productivity Commission, *National Disability Insurance Scheme (NDIS) Costs*.

53 half of the board members: Helen Dickinson, "A disabled NDIA chair is a great first move in the NDIS reset. Here's what should happen next", *The Conversation*, 27 September 2022. As well as a new chair, Kurt Fearnley, the NDIA also has a new CEO, Rebecca Falkingham. She has previously been secretary to the Victorian Department of Justice and Community Safety and is the first woman to hold the role permanently. Some people in the disability community have said this is a missed opportunity to appoint a person with a disability to this important role, and that it sends a negative message about the capacity of people with a disability to lead organisations that are centrally important to them.

54 political scientist Mark Considine: Considine, *The Careless State*.

54 "choice to voice": Mark Considine, "Choice versus voice: why money won't fix Australia's broken social services model", *Inside Story*, 22 June 2023, p. 3.

56 four dimensions: Sandra Fredman, "Substantive equality revisited", *International Journal of Constitutional Law*, vol. 14, no. 3, 2016, pp. 712, 714.

56 the need for structural change: *General Comment No 6: Equality and Non-Discrimination 2018* (CRPD/C/GC/6).

56 "To be misrecognized": Nancy Fraser, "Rethinking recognition", *New Left Review*, no. 3, May/June 2000.

Sana Nakata & Daniel Bray

Our home is a meeting place. Our families are the coming together of people from communities with long histories of conflict and division. Our sons can name the places of their *kulkulgal ateh*, their Maltese *nannu*, their German *oma*, and the grandmother they call *aka*. The conflicts and divisions our family lines represent are not metaphorical. War lingers in unexpected ways. Our ancestors stared down the barrels of each other's guns and starved each other, and we no longer live in the places any of them called home. Our love is an irreconcilable peace. It is not forged in the identification and priority of our likenesses, any more than race divides us. Our home is a meeting place because here these temporal and geographical trajectories interact in ways that are beautiful and hard and joyful and unexpected. We forget sometimes that not everyone lives here.

The trajectories of our lives have produced a differentiated commitment to democracy. Sana uses democratic principles as a way of holding the existing political system to account. She is not much invested in this democracy, given that so much violence and injustice has been done by the state to Aboriginal people and Torres Strait Islanders while Australia has called itself democratic. Her engagement with democratic theory is more along of the lines of, "well, if you wish to call yourself a democracy, perhaps you should be one." Daniel does not disagree with this, but points out the ways in which democratic principles, when sincerely practised, do lend themselves to achieving a more just world. Democratic principles can be effective tools for justice.

The national referendum on the proposal for an Aboriginal and Torres Strait Islander Voice to Parliament has focused our attention upon the different democratic grounds for supporting it. Three key claims are made: first, democracy is more than the aggregation of votes; second, the Voice addresses systemic and structural injustice; and third, renewal ensures that our democracy adapts to the changing fabric of society and politics. From one perspective, these arguments are grounded in a commitment to democracy. From another perspective, these arguments are grounded in a commitment to justice in a place where democracy has so far failed to deliver it.

These points are all made by Professor Davis at different points in her essay. We emphasise them here because as campaigning for and against the Voice to Parliament heats up, it is becoming apparent that one central argument of the No case is that the Voice will somehow undermine the democratic foundations of Australia. We want to highlight that this view relies upon an understanding of democracy that does not capture the values and practices of existing liberal democratic societies. It adopts an extraordinarily narrow conception of democracy that is, frankly, out of touch. It also wrongly presumes that democratic institutions and processes automatically operate to the benefit of all, when in fact they need to be designed to reflect the communities they govern. If one is genuinely committed to principles of equality, the rule of law and a fair go – to repeat the rhetoric of public naysayers – then there are fundamental democratic reasons to support the Voice, rather than to oppose it.

In short, we view the Voice to Parliament as a democratic imperative – expanding democratic representation, redressing structural injustice – and as a form of renewal by which our democracy responds to contemporary social and political conditions.

Opponents of the Voice often assert that a special advisory institution for Aboriginal people and Torres Strait Islanders undermines the democratic role of elected parliamentarians. This is to reduce democracy to the processes that elect parliamentary representatives and ensure their accountability through the ballot box. In fact, modern democratic politics involves a broader range of representative processes and practices through which diverse peoples and their political institutions are empowered to discuss, contest and decide the course of their common life together despite deep divisions and disagreements.

Democratic politics is more than the filling of parliamentary benches. Representative democracy demands more than a right to vote. Representation is a process mediated by a variety of actors and institutions – it includes the state, politicians and political parties, but also unions, lobbyists, NGOs, the media and protest movements – which together enable forms of political participation and contestation in which all members of a community can engage.

It is these broader processes of deliberation and contestation that expand representative politics beyond the ballot box and actualise democratic societies by meaningfully connecting parliaments and the people. Political theorist Nadia Urbinati writes in *Representative Democracy: Principles and Genealogy* that "the multiple sources of information and the varied forms of communication and influence that citizens activate through media, social movements and political parties set the tone of representation in a democratic society by making the social political. They are constitutive components of representation, not accessories." A Voice to Parliament does not supplant a much wider, more diverse field of Indigenous representation that takes place beyond the reaches of the colonial state. But it does expand that field specifically to facilitate the connection to political decision-making.

In this view, values that are integral to contemporary democracy include: the mechanisms of accountability citizens can exercise outside of elections; the deliberative capacity of political communication; the autonomy and impact of civil society; and importantly, the inclusion of affected people in policymaking and the empowerment of the historically marginalised. Seen from this vantage point, the Voice will enhance Australian democracy.

Although voting rights were incrementally accorded to Aboriginal people and Torres Strait Islanders from the 1960s, they have had very little effective political power and influence in the corridors of Canberra. Even as we see increasing numbers of Aboriginal members of parliament, we are reminded that each alone cannot represent all Aboriginal people and nor are they empowered to. Moreover, there are yet to be any Torres Strait Islander representatives at the Commonwealth level, and so we know that existing voting rights and political institutions alone cannot represent the interests of Aboriginal and Torres Strait Islander people to the federal government.

History has taught us that treating the most marginalised members of a society as we treat everybody else can be the source of their disadvantage. In pursuit of substantive equality, often we must treat people differently: we must consider the specific needs and histories of marginalised groups in order to create opportunities for them to participate in society. Special measures are justified when they empower historically and structurally marginalised groups to participate more fully and meaningfully in society. Such measures are not mechanisms that divide the country; rather, they work to bring people together by giving everyone a fair go.

In political communities made up of structurally disadvantaged peoples with unique experiences of the world, it is not only democratically legitimate but a fundamental democratic imperative to create specific mechanisms that redress this disadvantage. To do so deepens the democratic character of a nation and does not in any way diminish or reduce the rights of others.

Consequently, recognising the dispossession of this continent's First Peoples and rectifying the sustained marginalisation and disadvantage that the existing political system has delivered is the primary democratic justification for the Voice. As

Davis's essay reminds us, the stakes are high. Her essay does not enumerate exceptional failures, worst-case scenarios or outlier events. Her essay tells us that the torment of powerlessness – from child removals, burning communities to the ground, the gross mismanagement of the Indigenous Advancement Strategy and more – is Indigenous governance as it is designed to be. This is not a case of good intent gone awry, or benevolence misplaced; this is not a bad-apple bureaucrat, or a case of not doing better before we knew better. Structural injustice does not exist because we do not know our history or the truth. Structural injustice exists because that is how our political system is structured. We are getting exactly what the system was designed to deliver. A Voice to Parliament alone cannot specifically redress every injustice, but it will connect people to power in a way that currently does not happen. Democracy demands nothing less.

Democracy is an unfinished project, which must be continually renewed in the light of changed social conditions. John Dewey wrote that "Every generation has to accomplish democracy over again for itself . . . its very nature, its essence cannot be handed from one person or one generation to another, but has to be worked out in terms of the needs, problems and conditions of social life." The point is that the capacity of democracy to adapt itself in response to changes in the world, including changing social norms and attitudes, is part of what helps to keep democracies democratic: it supports plurality, not just within generations but across them, and in doing so guards against hegemonic concentrations of identity and authoritarian rule.

Those who argue that the safeguard of a democracy is its unchanging nature are wrong. Renewal is how nations inoculate themselves against new forms of division and conflict that emerge when the people and the power continue to diverge. This is exactly what constitutional reform to protect an Aboriginal and Torres Strait Islander Voice to Parliament works to achieve. The proposal for a Voice takes seriously the weaknesses of Australia's democracy and proposes a constitutional remedy. The Voice endows with a political power of representation a group that Australian democracy has marginalised – not by accident, but by design.

On lazy Sunday mornings, Sana's voice will become increasingly loud and argumentative: democratic renewal is not an analogy for Indigenous justice. It is not the job of Aboriginal and Torres Strait Islander communities to improve a political system that has failed us so consistently. Before Daniel can clarify that he is actually agreeing, and is only pointing out that the Voice remains a democratic imperative even if improving democracy isn't the end goal, our youngest child bursts in: "Please, don't fight!" Our children hear Mum and Dad vehemently agreeing about something from their different worldviews, their different ontological commitments. This is the meeting place. It is a place where even agreement is noisy. It is where common interests have sharp, broken edges. Where the peace is fragile. Where understanding is often incomplete. It is where the past and the present and the future converge in moments that seem like they should break us apart, but don't.

Sana Nakata & Daniel Bray

Mark McKenna

Voice of Reason is one of the most detailed and persuasive cases for the Voice I've encountered to date. Megan Davis has explained why the Voice is needed from the ground up. The examples she explores, sometimes in granular detail, highlight the failure of past policies and the urgent need for a constitutionally enshrined Indigenous Voice to the Commonwealth Parliament.

Davis also brings out the creative and imaginative dimensions of the Voice – both in its conception and its constitutional function. She explains why the Voice is an Indigenous and Australian solution to the complex historical and political circumstances faced by Aboriginal people. She also documents the long, tortuous journey to the referendum – pointing out that since 2011, we have witnessed seven public processes and ten public reports on constitutional recognition. As she laments, "at each meeting, for each prime minister, we had to explain the process from scratch."

Like the official "Case for Voting Yes," published online by the Australian Electoral Commission, and her recent publication with her UNSW colleague Professor George Williams – *Everything You Need to Know About the Voice* – Davis's essay is there for every Australian to read and understand. Just how many voters will take up these or other opportunities to cast an informed vote in the referendum is difficult to estimate. But for anyone seeking to persuade family, friends or their local communities to vote Yes – or, as Davis colourfully put it in a recent interview on *Late Night Live* to join the road to "Yes town" – *Voice of Reason* is essential reading. As it stands, the need for persuasive arguments and positive stories that illustrate the practical advantages of the Voice and constitutional change grows more pressing by the day.

On 26 June, the day *Voice of Reason* was published, Newspoll showed that support for the Voice had dropped below 50 per cent nationally, with only two states

(New South Wales and Victoria) registering more Yes than No voters. By late July, only three months out from the referendum, the same poll showed a continuing downward trend across the nation: 41 per cent Yes; 48 per cent No; 11 per cent undecided; and not one state recording over 50 per cent support for the Yes case.

As Australia enters the most crucial period of the referendum campaign, the fear of failure is palpable. The bar to achieve success inches ever higher. Calls to abandon the referendum have come from historian Bain Attwood, journalists, and Coalition MPs who feign concern for the future of reconciliation even though they did little during nine years of Coalition government to legislate the Voice or put forward a viable alternative to the proposed constitutional amendment. They cry out for detail at the same time as they provide no detail themselves. They argue that the Voice is divisive as they do all in their power to sow confusion and discord. They speak of their attachment to the constitution and argue the Voice will divide Australia on the grounds of race, when they know full well that racism is embedded in the very constitution they claim to protect.

Like the Nationals, Dutton's intention was always to scuttle the Voice. The only recognition he is willing to countenance is recognition on his own terms. Even more reason, then, not to abandon the referendum. After having achieved the momentous task of securing a referendum, turning back now would inevitably be seen as a de facto defeat, demoralise a generation of Indigenous leaders and hand an easy victory to the naysayers and scaremongers. In any case, Albanese has made it clear that he is not in office to mark time:

> I'm not here to occupy the space. To change who is in the white car. I'm here to change the country. And there's nowhere more important than changing the country than changing our nation's constitution to recognise the fullness of our history. So I want this done for Indigenous Australians but I want it done for all Australians. We will feel better about ourselves if we get this done ... Australia will be seen as a better nation as well by the rest of the world.

Albanese's words echoed those of Gough Whitlam when he launched Labor's election campaign at Blacktown Town Hall in December 1972: "All of us as Australians are diminished while the Aborigines are denied their rightful place in this nation."

To a large extent, the referendum campaign has pivoted on ideas that reflect an aversion to all things "political." In different ways — and there's certainly no equivalence between Dutton's anti-Canberra rhetoric and the Yes campaign's desire to take the discussion away from the political arena into local communities — both sides seek to distance themselves from politics. Like Morrison before him, Dutton, who presumably wants to be prime minister and believes in the transformative capacity of parliament, regurgitates cheap anti-Canberra rhetoric at every opportunity. While Senator Jacinta Price, whose office, like that of every parliamentarian, would not function without access to the informed and hopefully fearless advice of public servants, does all she can to besmirch the Canberra "bureaucracy." In any other workplace they would be sacked for damaging their employer's reputation.

For the Yes campaign, there's an obvious tightrope to walk: how to engage Labor and other members of parliament who have helped make the referendum a reality while repeatedly arguing that the referendum doesn't belong to politicians but to the Australian people. Davis, for example, places her faith in the new politics that emerged in the last federal election, one in which the major parties struggled to secure a primary vote above 30 per cent, while Greens and progressively inclined independents won an ever-increasing proportion of seats in electorates that were previously Liberal strongholds. "The demographics have changed," she argues, and "the politics have changed." True. Yet she also seeks to distance the Yes campaign from politics, claiming, perhaps rightly, that the referendum needs to "engage Australians on a higher level than political cynicism. The heart and the head. People, not politicians."

While the desire to "escape the political" seems to be the point on which all sides of politics agree, there is no escaping the fact that the referendum is an intensely political process. The very structure of a referendum, with its binary Yes and No alternatives, immediately implies that both cases have equal validity. No matter how misleading and vacuous the No-case arguments might be, they are validated merely by being seen as the alternative to the proposed constitutional amendment. Moreover, unlike the 1967 referendum, when there was no official No case, the 2023 referendum campaign is already captive to an adversarial political process. Like it or not, partisan politics has its paws all over the referendum. Even the Voice itself, if the referendum succeeds, will be tasked with managing the same political reality, and will obviously need to be conscious of its own political optics in such an intensely competitive and antagonistic political system.

For Albanese and Labor, there's a delicate task ahead. To what extent does the prime minister attempt to enter the fray? Is Albanese merely a facilitator of the debate? A leader who has done his bit by getting the referendum legislation through parliament and now hands it over to the Australian people? Or does he seek to lead? It's already evident that the No campaign has a clear leader: Opposition Leader Peter Dutton, backed by Warren Mundine and Senator Jacinta Price. But who is the leader of the Yes campaign? While a long list of names come to mind – from Albanese and Linda Burney to Noel Pearson, Megan Davis, Rachel Perkins, Marcia Langton and Thomas Mayo – there is no clear answer. Given the nature of the Yes strategy, perhaps a community campaign requires a community of leaders, but in the cut and thrust of adversarial politics, the "courageous leader" Davis speaks of would seem essential.

More broadly, the issue is not whether the referendum campaign is "political," but how its politics is conducted; how we, as voters, and politicians, as our representatives, engage in political discussion – whether inside or outside the parliament – and ensure that the spirit and character of the referendum debate improves the fabric of our democracy. After all, the Voice is an attempt to better inform the Commonwealth parliament on "matters relating to Aboriginal and Torres Strait Islander peoples," and to work with it constructively. There is little point in deriding politics and politicians when the Voice, or any future proposal for that matter, will rely on politicians for its efficacy.

To drive home the underlying urgency of the Voice, Davis draws perceptively on the history of invasion and dispossession to illustrate the marginal position in which Indigenous Australians find themselves today, especially in relation to the exercise of political power. Many of the progressive democratic reforms cherished by non-Indigenous Australians, often expressed through ideas such as the "fair go," emerged under White Australia, at a time when Aboriginal people were rendered invisible and excluded from the glorious narrative of democratic advancement. Democracy and equality were ideas treasured by British Australians, but they were also exclusive because they applied only to whites. Equally, the land that became "the great Australian dream" was taken from Indigenous Australians without treaty, compensation or consent.

This raises one of the key challenges for the Yes campaign. The referendum implicitly asks the vast majority of Australians to recognise and understand a different historical experience to their own; to recognise that, for Indigenous Australians, the history of the last 235 years has been far removed from the stories of peaceful progress that have comforted white Australians for so long. In other words, the referendum asks Australians to do what Prime Minister Paul Keating suggested in his Redfern Park speech in 1992: to imagine that "we" had suffered the "murders ... discrimination and exclusion." "With some noble exceptions," said Keating, "we failed to make the most basic human response ... to ask how would I feel if this were done to me? As a consequence, we failed to see that what we were doing degraded all of us."

When Peter Dutton stokes fear and anxiety by claiming that a constitutionally enshrined Voice will see the "greatest change" to our system of government since

Federation, he both wildly exaggerates the risks and fails spectacularly to demonstrate empathy. What of the changes forced on First Nations peoples by invasion and dispossession? What of the changes wrought by over two centuries of government policies designed to eradicate Aboriginal and Torres Strait Islander cultures and dictate every aspect of their peoples' lives? What of their long struggle for their rights? And what of their exclusion from the constitution?

In grave tones, Dutton warns Australians about a constitutional amendment that will genuinely and positively include Indigenous people in our constitution for the first time since 1901. He stresses the virtues of the constitution's stability and continuity. As he and others so often remind us, the constitution has "served Australia well." But who has it served well? And for whom has it provided "stability and continuity"?

Because of their exclusion from the nation's founding document, Indigenous Australians understand the Australian constitution far better than other Australians. They do not have the luxury of ignorance.

Over the past fifty years, the presence of Indigenous culture and history has become more visible in Australia's public culture; from Welcome to Country ceremonies, to place names, art, dance, music and literature, and the opening ceremonies of football finals, school assemblies and, since 2008, the opening of federal parliament after each federal election. For many Australians and certainly for visitors from overseas, this is the most distinctive aspect of Australian culture.

How long can Australians remain content to draw on this rich Indigenous knowledge and heritage as mere symbolism? Surely we have to give more; surely we need to demonstrate that we have listened to and heard Indigenous Australians by agreeing to establish what the Uluru Statement asked for: "the establishment of a First Nations Voice enshrined in the Constitution," which, as Davis argues, will constitute a "dialogue for time immemorial between the First Nations and the Australian people." This is the "constitutional moment" of reckoning that the coming referendum has placed before us.

In its tone and gracious request, the Uluru Statement from the Heart calls to mind previous invitations from Aboriginal and Torres Strait Islander peoples to their fellow citizens.

Among the thousands who walked across Sydney Harbour Bridge in May 2000, there were undoubtedly many reasons for attending. But the overwhelming expression of support for reconciliation would lodge permanently in the nation's memory. So too would the simple act of walking, which became one of the most powerful metaphors employed by Indigenous leaders when seeking support from their fellow Australians.

In October 1992, the Council for Aboriginal Reconciliation explained that the process of reconciliation "involves all of us walking together to find a better path to the future of this nation." In May 2017, the final words of the Uluṟu Statement from the Heart invited Australians "to walk with us in a movement of the Australian people for a better future."

I can only admire the optimism and determination of Davis and so many other Indigenous leaders, who continue to hold out their invitation to Australians to "walk" with them. As Davis argues, over the next three months, the Yes campaign needs to "explain to Australians why the Voice is needed."

The coming referendum is a once-in-a-lifetime opportunity to make the Voice work to the betterment of Indigenous Australians and the entire nation.

Mark McKenna

Antoinette Braybrook

"They do not listen because they do not have to." This quote from Yunupingu sets the scene for Megan Davis's thought-provoking Quarterly Essay. As Megan writes, that quote "succinctly summed up the problem" that has led to this year's referendum. And it resonated powerfully with me, an Aboriginal woman who has spent the past two decades working on the frontline of family violence, witnessing and personally experiencing the silencing of Aboriginal and Torres Strait Islander women.

Twenty years ago, I was instrumental in establishing Djirra together with a small group of like-minded Aboriginal women and men. I took on the role of inaugural CEO, and the passion and determination that fuelled me then remains to this day. Djirra is a specialist Aboriginal community-controlled organisation based in Victoria. Our team of around 100 work every day with Aboriginal and Torres Strait Islander people who experience or are at risk of experiencing family violence, predominantly women and their children.

In my twenty years on the frontline of Aboriginal women's safety I have seen and heard a lot. But before I elaborate on what those two decades have taught me – and the lessons that, I believe, might be drawn from them for those considering whether or not to support the Voice – it is important for me to say that I do not speak on behalf of anyone other than myself.

My authority to do what I do comes from being an Aboriginal woman with my own lived experience and the trust and confidence Aboriginal women place in me. My CEO title carries little weight in my Aboriginal world, but it makes sense and opens doors in the world of many reading this. I take my responsibility seriously, and it is with that in mind that I offer a deeply personal and considered response to Megan's essay. These are my own views, but I cannot deny that they are informed by my work.

I speak my truth here as an Aboriginal woman, knowing that I am exposed. This is not unusual in my work, but I am extremely conscious of the elevated hatred that has descended on all of us at this critical time as First Nations people: the extremist views, the white supremacy, the lateral violence – all of it not just attacking our personal safety, but also making media and social media platforms unsafe. Truth hurts, it's uncomfortable, but it must be spoken, written and heard.

Djirra's work is holistic, providing frontline legal, counselling and case management services, as well as our signature early intervention and prevention programs. Aboriginal women and their children who come to Djirra are seen, believed and respected. There is no test of cultural integrity, no doubting and no judgement. Through our work we keep Aboriginal women and their children's experiences and lived reality visible. We are fearless and unapologetic in our advocacy and continuously look for ways to break through the structural silencing and be heard. And let me tell you, that is not easy, with Aboriginal women's lived reality too often rendered all but invisible.

This can be seen in the National Plan to Reduce Violence Against Women that has guided work in this area for many years. This "mainstream" plan has not made a difference for Aboriginal women. During the twelve years of its existence – and over my twenty years as Djirra's CEO – I have only seen rates of violence against our women increase.

Reader, let me ask you two questions: Do you know that we have been advocating for many years for a standalone, self-determined National Plan to End Violence Against First Nations Women – one that does not apply a one-size-fits-all approach or render us invisible? Do you know that there is currently a Senate inquiry into missing and murdered First Nations women? It's very likely you don't, and there's a reason for that.

It has always been us, First Nations women, who have done the heavy lifting, who have been vocal and fervent, never silent, about the violence we experience from individuals from many cultures and backgrounds. We have not been silent about the systemic violence and racism we experience from government agencies and service providers, which sees our kids taken at alarming rates, our people achieve the abhorrent, heartbreaking record of being the most incarcerated people in the world, and our women's safety not prioritised and their lives compromised.

We continue to be silenced and disbelieved, but never silent. There's a difference.

Megan writes that "the need for the Voice is best articulated by Aboriginal people who have experienced voicelessness." I don't disagree, but I would make that point slightly differently and say that the need for the Voice is also best articulated by Aboriginal people who have been silenced and disbelieved.

This, too, has been my lived experience. In my twenty years working in family violence, I have been sidelined, shut out of important conversations and excluded. That is because what I have to say represents the real experiences of Aboriginal women and children. Because what I have to say makes some people uncomfortable. Because what I have to say is about Aboriginal women leading and determining for ourselves.

I have a deeply personal interest in change. I feel strongly that a successful referendum could be the game-changer that we so need. Cynical supporters of the "No" campaign talk about the change that's needed "on the ground." They politicise Aboriginal women and their children's safety. We have become a political football in this debate, something I find both disgusting and disheartening. They talk endlessly about the need for "practical change." Whatever do they mean by that? Is the change that we Aboriginal women seek and advocate for not "practical"? What could be more "practical" than saving Aboriginal women's lives?

Many of us have laboured for years to bear witness to what's happening "on the ground" and show the way forward. We have the solutions. We know what will make a difference. But we are not heard. We are not heard by those who need to listen, because, as Megan quotes Yunupingu, those who should be leaning in to hear our solutions "don't have to."

If they were listening, here's some of what they might hear.

The political handballing of Aboriginal and Torres Strait Islander issues between the federal and state governments must stop. It's time for national leadership to address the violence against our women and children, the high rates of child removal, the poor and unacceptable health status of our people and the high incarceration rates. It's time for our people to have a say in the policies and decisions that affect our lives. It's time.

Governments have long masked inaction through tokenistic symbolism that does not result in real change. As Megan writes, "Symbolic gestures matter until shit gets real." Shit has been "real" for our women and children since colonisation began.

Governments have controlled Aboriginal people through what Megan describes as "regulatory ritualism," another phrase that resonated deeply with me. As she explains, regulatory ritualism is "the acceptance of institutionalised means for securing regulatory goals while losing all focus on achieving the goals or outcomes themselves." I gave the Reconciliation Oration for the City of Melbourne earlier this year, and I spoke to this idea, though I didn't name it as such. I shared the perpetual cycle of key dates we go through year after year, from 26 January to the tabling of the Close the Gap report in parliament, to Reconciliation week, to the Sixteen Days of Activism Against Gender-Based Violence – all without seeing any real change.

In many ways, we as Aboriginal people may have become stuck in this cycle of government-imposed regulation and almost complicit in this regulatory ritualism, not by choice but because it's the only way we are able to elevate our voices. We participate in the inquiries and imposed government reviews and evaluations; some sit on the hand-picked advisory committees. Twenty years of living each year in the same way, knowing what's coming, is enough for me to say that something has to change.

We see this regulatory ritualism played out time and again through fickle and uncertain government funding patterns. Funding responsibility for Djirra and other Family Violence Prevention and Legal Services has shifted so many times without consultation – or engagement – that even to attempt a brief summary here is impossible. What I will say is that so much money goes unnecessarily – and unacceptably – into establishing new bodies, or to expanding government departments to administer and oversee funding of our services. It's money that does not hit the ground, money that keeps bureaucrats employed in high-paying roles, money that does not support services that give priority to Aboriginal women's safety.

Then there's the introduction by government and policy-makers of new ideas that mask the control and further regulation of us. You may have heard of "co-design" pitched as a way of working together to achieve a self-determined outcome. I am not convinced, especially given that the power imbalance between government and First Nations people remains.

I can honestly say that in decades of doing this we have been saying the same things over and over again, and we've seen very little change. We have made hundreds of recommendations to governments that are filed away and never considered. There has to be a better, fairer and more dignified way.

A successful referendum could break this pattern of regulatory ritualism, giving us a real and different kind of "voice," one that cannot be taken away by a change in government, an opportunity to speak that does not depend on the benevolence of white people working in the bureaucracy or white systems to offer us that "voice." It would be a voice that takes into account the unique and diverse cultures and experiences of First Nations people. They will finally listen because they "have to."

So, yes, I want change. Yes, it's time to make a difference. Yes, it's time to be heard. Yes, it's time for truth. Yes, it's time for a more equitable future. Yes, this could be a new chapter, not the last word. Yes, this is about trust. Yes, it's time for others to take responsibility and carry some of the load and feel privileged in doing so.

For me, it's yes.

Antoinette Braybrook

Daniel James

Megan Davis avoids the obvious choice, as a child of the 1980s, to find meaning in John Farnham's hit "You're the Voice," instead opting for "Age of Reason" – as someone with her impressive scholastic and legal background would, of course. But there is another Farnham song that could also describe the position we're in when it comes to the Voice: "Two Strong Hearts" – "reaching out forever like a river to the sea." The Uluru Statement from the Heart is another iteration of the offerings First Nations have made to the colonial state over the last two centuries – reaching out. Without the selfless advocacy of so many, Uluru would not have gained the traction it has. The country needed to change before it could be embraced.

The road to a referendum on a Voice has been long and arduous. In *Voice of Reason*, Davis flags the stations along that road. Initiatives and attitudes, some well-intentioned, some designed to destroy us. Despite the motives, good or bad, both have invariably failed to change the way of things for First Nations people under the shackles of the colonial experiment.

Colonialism engulfed us all. The survivors and fighters – from first contact to the earliest days of Federation and beyond – soon understood that the best way to resist and then change the new order was from within, no matter how painstaking or traumatic that was. Seeking an active role in the white democratic life of a country founded on the bodies of its original inhabitants was, and is, no easy task. To see it, as some critics do, as conformity is not only a gross insult to so many of our forebears, but also displays a rudimentary understanding of history and empathy. It also isn't a cessation of sovereignty; that was never ceded. Our land was stolen and our free movement across what was ours was restricted to the point of forbiddance.

It stands to reason, then, that to loosen its grip, to change the way modern colonialism influences the lives of First Nations communities, it will be necessary to change the founding document of this country and tend to the machinations of its parliament on issues pertinent to us in real time.

How much time have we lost along the way? Davis reminds us that for much of the 1990s and the early twentieth century the notion of reconciliation was essentially privatised. The Howard government washed its hands of reconciliation in its truest sense, finding greater comfort in stoking the tedious history wars and promulgating a Python-esque view of the benefits of colonialism for First Nations people.

It fed into that government's emphasis on "practical reconciliation," a political inertia after *Mabo* and *Wik* which gave birth to the Reconciliation Action Plan – a dubious velvet-covered instrument that only reckons with activities designed to highlight progress through the number of boxes ticked. As Davis writes, "[the RAP] focuses on private action or corporate civic action, and not on truth and justice." It's perhaps why corporate Australia, including the not-for-profit sector, so fervently adopted RAPs – as an easy way to cleanse collective guilt by doing the bare minimum, without addressing truth and justice, without doing the heavy lifting of reconciliation. It reminds us that true reconciliation is looking forward and looking back, realising the tense of all things coexisting and shaping all of us in any given moment. The long view through mature eyes, just as our old people tried to instil in us.

The ultimate disconnect is not the rationale for a Voice, especially if one considers all that has come before. No, the real stumbling block for people considering whether to support it or not is whether they can muster enough faith in the political system and its operatives at a time when faith in public institutions and those who run them has never been more tenuous. Anyone who is even a part-time student of the blak struggle in all its guises knows that the advocates, the leaders, the voices from communities around Australia will throw themselves earnestly and honestly into the task of speaking truth to power.

What is far less certain is the will of political leaders of all persuasions to hear the truth and act upon it. All it takes is one John Howard or one of his political spawn to arrest the legitimacy of truth-telling. It's why enshrinement of the Voice in the constitution and not merely through legislation is important.

In her concluding paragraph, Davis challenges us: "We Aboriginal people must suspend our belief that the system cannot change. We must suspend our belief that the nation cannot change." I think it requires more than that – it's going to take a leap of faith. Even once First Nations people avail themselves of all the arguments around the Voice, as many have, that final act of faith is hard to approach, let alone make. It's why so many are still undecided in my community: their reasons are valid, their hesitancy understandable. I pondered this final step for a long time myself before taking it.

As I write this, the Melbourne Remand Centre, with a capacity of close to 600, currently houses 143 Aboriginal male prisoners. Almost every Victorian Aboriginal person with ongoing connections to this part of the colony would know, or know of, First Nations people in prison. You can't help but understand why there is a resistance among many of us to dealing with the state, let alone entering into dialogue with it. Yet this is again what is on offer; one side has shown heart, demonstrated vulnerability through strength. Will the broader community reveal its own heart? Because that's what it's going to take if we're to break the status quo.

Daniel James

Damien Freeman

Few people have been as invested in the forthcoming referendum as Megan Davis. She has been a protagonist in every key scene of the drama of constitutional recognition that has played out over the past two decades. In *Voice of Reason*, Davis reminds us of that journey, and of how much is at stake – not only for her personally but for Aboriginal and Torres Strait Islander people at large and, indeed, the whole country at this year's referendum.

No one who reads this essay can be left in any doubt about the crucial role she has played or what has motivated her. Central to the essay is her account of how the proposal for an Aboriginal and Torres Strait Islander Voice was developed; how it obtained the imprimatur of Indigenous consensus and, subsequently, parliamentary acceptance, so that it could ultimately be put to the electors at a referendum. This narrative is situated within Davis's analysis of the massive failures in public policy when it comes to Indigenous affairs and her own attempts at helping to identify problems and recommend solutions.

This experience allows her to assert with confidence that public policy and law reform will not improve unless a new mechanism is established to enable policy and lawmakers to hear Indigenous voices. She explains that this mechanism won't be effective, however, unless its existence is guaranteed by the Australian Constitution. Hence, the need for constitutional recognition not only of Aboriginal and Torres Strait Islander peoples but of the Aboriginal and Torres Strait Islander Voice. It is only in this way that "the torment of our powerlessness" can be ended. Thus, the heading "recognition and reconciliation" only appears halfway through the essay. For Davis and those who have toiled with her, the referendum proposal is primarily about addressing the failure of public policy in Indigenous affairs by entrenching a new consultative mechanism in the Constitution. Only by achieving this can reconciliation between Indigenous and non-Indigenous people occur, through the symbolic moment of amending the Constitution to recognise Indigenous people.

Within months of the publication of Davis's essay, the country will have voted either for or against the proposal she first read out at Uluṟu six years ago. When she was writing the essay, most electors were only just starting to become aware that they would have to vote for or against the proposal for a Voice to Parliament. So it is timely to think about what might be going through their minds.

Towards the beginning of her essay, Davis references Noel Pearson's claim in his 2022 Boyer Lectures that Aboriginal people remain the "most unloved" people in Australia. She writes that "Pearson's theory will be tested in 2023." Davis claims that Pearson's thesis applies to "an Old Australia," and that it is this Old Australia that is propping up the No campaign. She writes: "Conservatives are busy carving out a convenient narrative for themselves that there is a reasoned and respectable case for 'No'; there isn't." She continues by quoting Niki Savva's opinion that "While it is not true to say that every Australian who votes No in the Voice referendum is a racist, you can bet your bottom dollar that every racist will vote No."

I offer no comment about who is racist or how racists will vote. I do note, however, that – although I don't agree with them – there are principled reasons for voting No, as Greg Sheridan explains in a paper he wrote recently for the Centre for Independent Studies. His philosophical objections to the proposal do not make him racist and they are not misinformation – they are arguments that can and should be refuted. While Davis claims that conservatives are busy carving out a convenient narrative for voting No, some of us have spent the better part of a decade carving out the conservative case for voting Yes. I helped edit two collections of essays – *The Forgotten People: The liberal and conservative case for recognising Indigenous people* (2016) and *Statements from the Soul: The moral case for the Uluru Statement from the Heart* (2023) – which show that some conservatives are in fact motivated by their conservatism to vote "Yes" and to make the case for change. The case for change has never been confined to the purview of progressives. Conservatives since Edmund Burke have understood the need for change, and the proposal that is currently before us is one that owes much to conservative thought.

There is widespread acceptance among conservatives and progressives alike that Australia's Indigenous people should be recognised in the Constitution, just as there is widespread acceptance that public policy is failing badly when it comes to Indigenous affairs. The question is whether there will also be widespread acceptance by referendum day that a Voice will improve public policymaking in Indigenous affairs and similar acceptance that entrenching a Voice is the right way to recognise Indigenous people in the Constitution.

To achieve the requisite level of acceptance, electors need to feel comfortable that they understand, first, how a Voice could work and, second, why a Voice that works in that way will improve the lives of people on the ground. Sean Gordon, in his speech to the Sydney Institute last year, addressed this when he said, "As a nation, we all want to see more Indigenous communities driving a responsibilities agenda and leading change. There are pockets of change happening, but this change is slow. To accelerate progress, communities need to be able to tell government how to get rid of the barriers to their development, and they need a structure or group who is authorised to drive place-based reform. The Voice to Parliament can be that change if the Parliament designs it as such."

Greg Craven and I argue along similar lines in a paper we wrote this year for the Centre for Independent Studies, *Guaranteeing a Grassroots Megaphone: A centre-right approach to hearing Indigenous voices*. As we explain: "If the Indigenous Voice is designed as a grassroots megaphone, it will be something that conservative and liberal voters can support. We can all get behind a mechanism that enables people in Indigenous communities to provide advice to the Commonwealth Parliament about laws relating to Indigenous affairs. And we can all get behind the idea that, in light of Australia's history, the Constitution should guarantee that, in future, Indigenous voices will be heard before Parliament exercises its power to make laws with respect to Indigenous affairs."

More recently, Gavin Brown, a Wiradjuri man, authored PwC Indigenous Consulting's report entitled *Who Is Speaking? Who Is Listening? The architecture for creating a Voice as a vehicle for practical partnerships*. The report notes that the co-design report commissioned by the Morrison government and delivered in July 2021, known as the Calma/Langton report, dealt largely with the question of who is speaking at local, regional and national levels. It was focused on the Indigenous voices. To explain how the Voice will work in practice, the PwC report identifies the need also to consider who is listening to these voices, and the bridge between those doing the speaking and the way the parliament and the executive would listen. Brown notes that the desire for Indigenous peoples to be heard is a call for mutual respect and recognition. "Underpinning this structural reform is both the right to be heard, and the responsibility to speak. Rather than seeing the Voice as a threat to our democratic process, a well-designed structure which provides for local, regional and national input can actually be a crucial enabler for improving outcomes for Indigenous peoples," he says.

The value of the report lies in the way it explains the structural link between local and regional Voices and the national Voice. It explains that the local Voices will provide the critical power base for the parliament and the executive to engage successfully with Indigenous communities. The efficacy of the national Voice lies in the architecture that it provides for facilitating constructive engagement between these people on the ground and decision-makers in Canberra. It does this by creating a bridge – an institutional framework that ensures disempowered people can speak effectively to those with the power to make decisions, and that those decision-makers can listen effectively to what is being said.

Opponents of the Voice argue it risks being stacked with activists or, worse, people from the so-called Canberra bubble. Once you see the functions and the responsibilities of the Voice through this grassroots-up architecture, it seems unlikely this would occur, given the lines of accountability back to community.

Davis concludes her essay by relating how she has sought to reassure Indigenous people who feel cynical about the capacity of government to address their concerns that there is a better way of doing business, that their aspirations will be realised if we ensure that their voices are heard by law and policymakers. Their cynicism is understandable, and Davis has done our country a great service by patiently acknowledging and addressing it. But theirs is not the only cynicism that needs to be addressed. We need to explain to non-Indigenous electors who feel cynical about a Voice that a Voice that enables local Indigenous communities to work with policymakers to find solutions to the problems that beset their communities will bring about solutions that enable Indigenous communities to take responsibility for their own prosperity.

That non-Indigenous electors might be cynical about the ability of a Voice to address the plight of many of their Indigenous compatriots does not necessarily mean they do not love Aboriginal people. A different interpretation could be that, in a constitutionally conservative nation, electors need to understand what they are being asked to vote for and why it will help improve the lives of people on the ground. If this is explained to them, they will vote Yes in large numbers and will affirm their love of their fellow Aboriginal citizens.

Damien Freeman

Rachel Buchanan

Back in 2001, the literary journal *Meanjin* was preparing a special issue called "Poetics" and selected writers were invited to record their poems to a CD (ironically titled *Enhancer*) that would be sold with the journal, tucked into a plastic pocket at the back.

I was asked to go to a place in Coburg or Brunswick, somewhere miles away from where I lived in Melbourne's west, and read "The Immigration Experience," a two-part piece about what the title says.

When I got there, Lisa Bellear was at the mic. I had heard of Bellear from the "Koorie survival show" that used to be on 3CR, a community radio station in Melbourne. Lisa read two powerful short poems – "Reconciliation Spins My Head" and "Prepared to Die" – in a voice that was slow and dreamy, edged with menace.

Then Lisa hung around to watch me. I was nervous. As I reflected in an essay for *Te Pouhere Kōrero*, the journal of the Māori Historians Association, I had not imagined what a Koorie person would think of my work. I had written my piece with a white Australian audience in mind, I guess, and maybe a Pākehā one as well.

Afterwards, we had a chat. Lisa was a warm person with a beautiful smile. She commented on my outfit – a subtle combo of a bright-orange fake-fur maternity dress worn over striped bell-bottomed leggings – and noted that we had both made mention of cousins in our work. I felt her reference was rather more sophisticated than mine but whatever. Then Lisa got to the point.

"We don't like it when you Māoris come over here and tell us how things should be for us," she said. Lisa was looking away from me as she spoke. Her voice was light, almost joking, but I heard her message. Do not speak for me. Do not compare your people with mine. Be respectful. Listen. Don't ever forget who you are and where you are.

Five years later, Lisa Bellear — poet, playwright, photographer, comedian — died in her sleep and the obituary published in The Age said 1000 people attended her funeral at the Victorian Aboriginal Advancement League headquarters in Thornbury.

This might sound weird, but I've learnt that it is a gift when someone important — say, Lisa Bellear — decides you are worth dressing down, and after reading Megan Davis's brilliant essay, this encounter with Lisa came back to me.

In arguing for a constitutional Voice, Davis says Australians "could see an unconventional yet compelling invitation to address one of the most acute challenges for Indigenous Australia: *getting the government to listen.*"

The second section of Davis's essay is called "The Torment of Our Powerlessness," a title not easy to forget. "Parliaments do not listen because they do not have to," Davis writes.

Bob Hawke promised a treaty (1988). Didn't happen. Royal Commissions have come and gone — Deaths in Custody (1991) and Little Children Are Sacred (2007) — but still nothing changed. The Northern Territory set up a Treaty Commission (2019) but the work fizzled out. South Australia announced treaty negotiations (2016), then a new government canned them. Now they are back on. A change of government in Victoria could derail the work happening here too.

As Davis said in her 2021 Mabo Oration: "Treaties that are not premised on the country's federal structure are not binding treaties."

Pandered to, placated, patted on the back, fobbed off with "Acknowledgments of Country and an endless parade of posters and water bottles and wristbands" or Reconciliation Action Plans (yesterday's news), Davis damns the ritualistic ways that federal, state and territory governments have signalled "connection and deep engagement" with First Nations communities while continuing to ignore what these communities are actually saying.

Attending a NAIDOC morning tea might make non-Aboriginal people living in Australia feel good, but it does nothing to reduce the numbers of First Nations children who are removed from their homes or the number of First Nations people who are in prison. (I mention child protection because Davis uses it as a case study to justify the need for a Voice to Parliament, and here in Victoria the Yoorrook Justice Commission's first inquiries have been on child protection and the criminal justice system.)

I understand some of the struggles here because I've seen similar ones at home. No matter what some people like to say, Aotearoa New Zealand is not a bicultural paradise where the immense harm of colonisation is being undone, one treaty settlement at a time. If that were so, why are so many of us here?

One in five Māori, about 170,000 people, live in Australia. In total, just under 560,000 New Zealand–born people live here, making us the fourth-largest immigrant community, behind people born in the United Kingdom, India and China.

Some of us refer to Australia as Te Ao Moemoea, which could mean the land of dreams or the land of the Dreaming, and even though we arrived as uninvited guests, this country has welcomed us. Australia has certainly been good to me. I have received an excellent tertiary education here, raised three kids with a top bloke (Italian-Anglo Australian), written four books, had good jobs and made good friends, but I also know my place.

Yes, I am an indigenous person in New Zealand, but, as Lisa Bellear reminded me all those years ago, here I am a migrant, a guest, a surface person wrapped in the blanket of my ancestry, a thin covering compared with the luxurious cloak First Nations people wear, the one created by 60,000 years of occupation, custodianship and care.

I am in awe of Professor Megan Davis, Aunty Pat Anderson AO and their many colleagues for the innovative and dogged work they did leading up to Uluṟu and what they've done since then. I am inspired by the fire and dignity of Professor Eleanor Bourke and the other Yoorook commissioners as they hold the state of Victoria to account in a series of extraordinary hearings (you can watch them online) and by the passion of many Elders who have chosen to give evidence so far.

Thank you for sharing your Country with me and my family. Thank you for your power, humility, generosity and intellectual, artistic, creative and legal excellence. I will vote Yes and I hope every other eligible Māori and Pākehā person living on your land does too.

Rachel Buchanan

Henry Reynolds

Megan Davis's *Voice of Reason* makes a significant contribution to the intensifying debate about the forthcoming referendum. It is a rational and persuasive account of the process of national consultation which culminated in the Uluṟu Statement from the Heart in May 2017. It provides a cogent account of the legal and political framework against which the 250 delegates negotiated their three-part program of Voice, truth-telling and treaty.

But, like in practically all the literature produced by either side of the debate, there is little about the international context. The debate is both contentious and notably parochial, even though for sixty years global opinion and international law have played major roles in the evolution of Australian politics and law. Some brief background may be necessary.

The Indigenous and Tribal Populations Convention, 1957 (No. 107) was the first international document which dealt specifically with the rights of indigenous people. Surprisingly, it had an almost immediate influence in Australia. Copies were distributed at the inaugural meeting of the Federal Council for the Advancement of Aborigines in Adelaide in 1958 and it was formally adopted a year later. Although assimilationist in tone, it strongly supported land rights. It was here that both Gough Whitlam and Don Dunstan received their inspiration for their pioneer land rights legislation in the Northern Territory and South Australia. The Murray Island land rights claim survived Queensland's challenge in *Mabo v Queensland no. 1* due to the anti-discrimination legislation of 1975, which drew on the UN's Convention of 1966. In his leading judgment in 1992, Justice Brennan declared that Australian courts had to keep the common law in step with international law and "neither be nor be seen to be frozen in an age of racial discrimination." He referred to both UN conventions and judgments of the International Court of Justice.

The political and constitutional rights of indigenous people were further developed in ILO Convention 169 of 1989, which both recognised and supported "the aspirations of these peoples to exercise control over their own institutions, ways of life and economic development and to maintain and develop their identities, languages and religions, within the framework of the States in which they live."

By then negotiations were underway at the UN, which eventually resulted in 2007 in the vote of a massive majority in the General Assembly in favour of the Declaration of the Rights of Indigenous People, to which Australia gave its formal support in 2009. The Declaration recognised and reaffirmed that indigenous peoples "possess collective rights which are indispensable for their existence, well-being and integral development as peoples." They also have the right of self-determination and "by virtue of that right they freely determine their political status and freely pursue their economic, social and cultural development." As well, they have the right to "autonomy or self-government in matters relating to their internal and local affairs."

The relevance of these international principles and standards for our current debate scarcely needs emphasising. It is surely strange that they are so rarely referred to. It suggests the advocates for the Yes case decided it was better not to mention the UN, international law or global opinion. Whether that was a prudent decision remains to be seen.

Henry Reynolds

Megan Davis

Each of the erudite responses to my Quarterly Essay stands on its own as worthy and incisive commentary on the essay and on this historic moment that we are barrelling towards. I make only a few observations in response. Sana Nakata and Daniel Bray's extraordinary contribution should be compulsory for all "undecideds." It should be read by the multitudinous commentators prosecuting the idea that Australian democracy and liberalism require no adjustment and no reform, and cannot recognise "difference" in a way that won't violate formal equality. If we set to one side that Australia is a nation that has enabled communities of different wealth to flourish because of a commitment to substantive equality, not formal equality, Bray and Nakata provide a sharp retort to those essentialists.

Their dialogue reminds me of the fascinating and sophisticated conversations that occurred in the First Nations Regional Dialogues. They were fierce and moving and messy and clever. Full of tears and anger and hope and covering the full spectrum of human emotion. For, you see, we were asked to talk to members of communities who are the end users of a billion-dollar industry that is so large and unaccountable that even the Productivity Commission can't track it. And we rock up to talk about the constitution over three days?

When Aunty Pat Anderson went on ABC TV's 7.30 to explain the dialogues, she spoke of the process as being just that – teary and angry – but the next day News.com.au had a headline: "People were angry: Uluru Statement architect weighs in on dialogues amid 'reparations', treaty controversy." Mainstream media see the dialogue participants and advocates for Uluru as angry activists with angry motives. It is so clichéd. What we saw, as Bray and Nakata elegantly put it, was a "meeting place. A place where even agreement is noisy."

> It is where common interests have sharp, broken edges. Where the peace is fragile. Where understanding is often incomplete. It is

where the past and the present and the future converge in moments that seem like they should break us apart, but don't.

This is the parliament.
This is Australian democracy.
This will be the Voice.

I see Bray and Nakata's concluding words as a neat metaphor for the Voice and for Australian democracy. Democracy should be the meeting place of all citizens. But for so long it hasn't been that for the First Peoples because, as they say, the marginalisation of First Peoples has been done "not by accident, but by design."

Nakata and Bray traverse some of that history. But more importantly, they explain that democratic governance, like our constitution, is not intended to be static, to stand still. As Bray and Nakata say:

> Those who argue that the safeguard of a democracy is its unchanging nature are wrong. Renewal is how nations inoculate themselves against new forms of division and conflict that emerge when the people and the power continue to diverge. This is exactly what constitutional reform to protect an Aboriginal and Torres Strait Islander Voice to Parliament works to achieve. The proposal for a Voice takes seriously the weaknesses of Australia's democracy and proposes a constitutional remedy.

After all, the origins of the parliament come from the post–Norman conquest formation of assemblies to talk. *Parler* is the French word for "to speak"– from which the word *parliament* evolved. And this is what dialogue seeks to do. It seeks to speak "to" the parliament and "to" the executive. Our parliamentary system is adversarial and is built upon the mediation of two versions of the good life. But for First Nations people, our world, our lives, our needs fall outside that spectrum because we are distinct cultural groups. The Voice is utterly consistent with our legal and political traditions, as it aligns with the values that Bray and Nakata show are integral to contemporary democracy, and this includes the mechanisms of accountability citizens can exercise outside of elections and the deliberative capacity of political communication and the inclusion of affected people in policymaking and the empowerment of the historically marginalised. We are asking to be listened to. That's all.

Bray and Nakata say, as we do, "From this vantage point, the Voice will enhance Australian democracy."

Damien Freeman sets up a straw man. I don't say that undecided non-Indigenous voters who have genuine questions about the Voice's ability to address the plight of Aboriginal people don't love Aboriginal people. I said Noel Pearson's claim that we are "unloved" will be tested at this referendum.

Freeman also says that Aboriginal cynicism is not the only cynicism that needs to be addressed and that we need to make the case to non-Indigenous electors who feel cynical about a Voice.

My entire work post-Uluṟu has been to turn up, tirelessly, to a host of different forums across Australia and write in different media to try to reach those people and explain how the Voice is and was expressly conceived, and has been developed, as a form of recognition that will be more than symbolism, that will help improve the lives of people on the ground. Unlike Freeman, most communities don't use the term "local communities" – that's not how they describe themselves. It's a bureaucratic term. It's a term used by the United Nations which has seen the diminution of Indigenous rights. They don't make a distinction between local communities and national voice. That's an artificial distinction: their Voice is their Voice no matter where the meeting place. They view this mechanism as grassroots communities wanting a Voice directly to Canberra, where national decisions are made. And most dialogues wanted to elect spokespeople directly via ballot-box elections. The design phase that the Labor government has committed to that follows a successful referendum will allow communities to contribute to that design. The one point they all made was that there is no existing entity or framework that represents their voice.

Freeman worries about me convincing cynical voters who don't know what the Voice will achieve. The Uluṟu Dialogues, which I co-chair with Pat Anderson, are on the ground every day doing the hard work of talking to cynical undecided and No voters, as well as to ATSI peoples and Yes voters. My team over six months in 2023 has been to Cooktown, Laura, Cairns, Mossman, Port Douglas, Kuranda, Ingham, Innisfail, Lightning Ridge, Walgett, Coonabarabran, Narrabri, Moree, Townsville, Palm Island, Eagleby, Broken Hill, Mudgee, Wellington, Gilgandra, Trangie, Narromine, Gulargambone, Nyngan, Warren, Lithgow, Wagga Wagga, Redfern, Nowra, Cairns, Mareeba, Tully, Brewarrina, Logan Central, Taree, Port Macquarie, Tamworth, Hervey Bay, Dubbo, Orange, Sydney, Newcastle and Logan City. We are soon moving to South Australia. We run small, face-to-face dialogues with Aussies and local Indigenous groups, some together, some separate. We have no "Yes" placards. We are there to educate, not proselytise.

What we are hearing is not cynicism about the Voice, or even opposition to the Voice, but voters with cynicism because the system does not work for them. They demonstrate little faith in Australia's democracy or Australia's politicians or Australian parliaments.

Freeman challenges me to persuade those voters, but neglects to consider an avalanche of misinformation and disinformation that's being driven by his side of politics (though definitely not by Freeman). If Australians thought the same way as LNP conservatives, the conservative vote would not have plummeted to the low thirties in the 2022 election. It's disappointing that they are now gleefully and publicly saying they will use this referendum and the lives of vulnerable First Nations communities to position themselves for the next election. It explains why a Voice is needed. It explains why the Uluṟu Statement was issued to the Australian people. Politicians only have their eyes on the three-year term. And for a party that is struggling to fundraise, the LNP sees this referendum as a money-making opportunity for themselves. That brazen pursuit of power is what I'm hearing as we travel the country talking to ordinary Aussies. Their cynicism is fuelled by retail Australian politics. And the more they hear about the Uluṟu Statement as an invitation issued to them, not to politicians, the more likely they are to vote Yes.

Daniel James addresses this from the Indigenous side of things in his eloquent reply. I have thought about the same issues he has written about for years and years. The deep concern of some of our people is that we do distrust the system because it's let us down so much. Even so, I do believe the 83 per cent statistic and the higher statistic from Reconciliation Australia that around 88 per cent of our mob support this. Because we are pragmatic people. We decided not to waste this opportunity. But we are all nervous. We are all anxious. The day after a referendum, if the result is No, all First Nations people will feel profoundly rejected by a system imposed on them, that they sought to join in an ever so modest way: Recognition Through a Voice. As Aunty Pat Anderson said on 7.30, "We are fringe dwellers," "We are knocking on the door." Will Australians open the door?

Which makes the Voice as a model and the Uluṟu invitation so remarkable: that after everything that has come before, we offer a modest constitutional option. The Voice is about listening. And constitutionally, it is about listening always. I found James's essay profoundly moving. Our people are taking a leap of faith. And they've placed that faith not in politicians but in their fellow Australians.

Henry Reynolds asks whether it was the right decision not to use international principles and standards for the current Voice debate. He writes, "It is surely strange that they are so rarely referred to. It suggests the advocates for the Yes case decided it was better not to mention the UN, international law or global opinion. Whether that was a prudent decision remains to be seen."

Reynolds need ask no more. If he reads the Referendum Council report, he can see that the process was influenced by international principles and standards. From

UNDRIP to CERD, it was influenced by the standards applicable to Australia. It also references many of the international resolutions on truth-telling.

However, where the UN is mostly referred to in this campaign is in No forums and campaign material seeding disinformation and misinformation on Facebook. I've been asked a number of times at community forums whether the Voice means the UN takes over Australia. I believe this referendum demonstrates the problem that can occur in liberal democracies where civics is poorly understood, and in particular it highlights the failure to educate about modern history and Australia's place in a global world. The UN conspiracies I am seeing and hearing align with the anti-WHO, anti-vaccine discourse that emerged in the COVID-19 pandemic.

Mark McKenna is the historian who influenced my thinking and my career turn to become an academic. His work on the 1999 referendum had a profound impact on how I thought about the republic referendum and Indigenous recognition. A failed Voice referendum will make it that much harder for a republic referendum. I do wonder, however, whether the legislative changes that needed to happen for the Voice referendum – such as fact-checking the pamphlets – will happen following this referendum.

Many Australians ask how the Voice will make a difference: read Antoinette Braybrook. There is no area that suffered more under nine years of conservative government than the field of family/domestic violence and violence against Indigenous women. When the Abbott government introduced the Indigenous Advancement Strategy and ripped $500 million out of community programs and policies, many of these were schemes, bodies and programs aimed at combating violence against Indigenous women. The conservatives pulled money for night patrols.

Braybrook talks about the silence and disbelief. We heard this a lot in the dialogues. The way the bureaucracy and executive in successive conservative governments ran Indigenous affairs was like some Florentine patronage scheme. If you're in the "in crowd," you'll be fine. If not, you're done until there's a change of government – and even then it's not guaranteed. The Australian National Audit Office reports provide a snapshot of the arbitrariness of executive decision-making. The picture is bleak for many. And the bureaucratic trend of co-design and sharing decision-making is so utterly ludicrous in a system where the power imbalance is acute for all but for a very few elite figures who, for various reasons, carve out their own boutique space.

Aboriginal and Torres Strait Islander women lead our communities. They do the heavy lifting. And our women are never silent. We are always talking up. The Voice is a mechanism that will allow many women and girls to flourish. One of the design principles that make up the detail is that the Voice must comprise equal numbers of men and women. This is critical. Constitutions do provide the material conditions for a dignified human life. It's in plain sight that the constitution has benefited Australians. But it has not benefited all. This referendum is about the Australian people agreeing that there is dignity in having a seat at the table and this will mean empowering women structurally.

My essay straddles an interesting phase in the referendum. It was published when Yes was ahead in the polls. That is no longer the case. But curiously, there are huge numbers of undecideds – somewhere near 40 per cent. I don't think anyone expected the misinformation and disinformation to dominate in the way it has. As *The Guardian* has reported, the No campaign even has funding and expertise from companies registered in Texas who are from the Christian far right and are experts in Trumpian misinformation and disinformation. The Yanks have arrived on our shore and they are interfering in the integrity of our democracy. This should be a bigger topic of conversation than it is. But will all these problems be cleaned up after the referendum?

I've led this work for seven years, maybe twelve if I start with Gillard's expert panel. I did not think that just months before the referendum the headline in *The Australian* would be "Prime Minister defends the length of the Uluṟu Statement." Ludicrous. While the political elites play political games, the issues that plague our community remain hidden from view. That's the tactic. If we are distracted from our jobs, then fewer Australians hear about the exigency of the Voice and why it is a clever and fair way to address a structural injustice. The exclusion of First Nations is not by accident but by design in the Australian constitution. I'll leave Bray and Nakata with the last word on this:

> Structural injustice exists because that is how our political system is structured. We are getting exactly what the system was designed to deliver. A Voice to Parliament alone cannot specifically redress every injustice, but it will connect people to power in a way that currently does not happen. Democracy demands nothing less.

Megan Davis

Antoinette Braybrook is the founding CEO of Djirra, an Aboriginal community-controlled organisation providing support to Aboriginal people experiencing family violence. She is also co-chair of Change the Record and played a key role in the campaign for a National Plan to End Violence Against First Nations Women. Between 2011 and 2022, she was the inaugural elected chairperson of the National Family Violence Prevention Legal Services Forum.

Rachel Buchanan (Taranaki, Te Ātiawa) lives on Bunurong land. Her latest book, *Te Motunui Epa*, was co-winner of the 2023 Ernest Scott Prize for History. Rachel was a finalist in the Māori Literature Trust's inaugural Keri Hulme Award.

Megan Davis is Professor of Constitutional Law at UNSW, a global Indigenous rights expert on the UN Expert Mechanism on the Rights of Indigenous Peoples, and a former chair of the UN Permanent Forum on Indigenous Issues. She was the first person to read out the Uluṟu Statement from the Heart, at Uluṟu in May 2017.

Damien Freeman is the principal policy adviser at the PM Glynn Institute, Australian Catholic University. His books include *Abbott's Right: The conservative tradition from Menzies to Abbott* and *Killer Kramer: Dame Leonie — a woman for all seasons*.

Daniel James is a Yorta Yorta man based in Melbourne. He won the 2018 Horne Prize for his essay *Ten More Days*. He also hosts The Mission on 3RRR FM. His debut novel will be published by Affirm Press.

Micheline Lee's novel *The Healing Party* was shortlisted for several awards, including the Victorian Premier's Literary Award. Born in Malaysia, she migrated to Australia when she was eight. Micheline has lived with a motor neurone disability from birth. She is also a former human rights lawyer and painter.

Mark McKenna is one of Australia's leading historians, based at the University of Sydney. He is the author of several prize-winning books, including *From the Edge: Australia's lost histories*, *Looking for Blackfellas' Point* and *An Eye for Eternity: The life of Manning Clark*, which won the Prime Minister's Literary Award for non-fiction and the Victorian, New South Wales, Queensland and South Australian premiers' awards.

Sana Nakata is a Torres Strait Islander and Principal Research Fellow at the Indigenous Education and Research Centre at James Cook University. **Daniel Bray** is Senior Lecturer in International Relations at La Trobe University. They work and write together on childhood and democratic theory.

Henry Reynolds is the author of many groundbreaking works of history, including *The Other Side of the Frontier*, *This Whispering in Our Hearts*, *Why Weren't We Told?*, *The Law of the Land* and recently *Truth Telling: History, sovereignty and the Uluru Statement*.

Milton Keynes UK
Ingram Content Group UK Ltd.
UKHW050733130923
428582UK00006B/14